# HIGH-PERFORMANCE
# HANDLING FOR STREET OR TRACK

## By Don Alexander

motorbooks

Library of Congress Cataloging-in-Publication data

Alexander, Don, 1948-
High-performance handling for street or track / Don Alexander.
    p. cm.
Summary: "Turn your daily driver, weekend fun ride, or track car into a corner-carving performance machine. From planning a course of modifications to installing parts to tuning handling characteristics, High-Performance Handling for Street or Track will have you cranking out high-g cornering forces on your favorite twisty course. Topics covered in High-Performance Handling for Street or Track include: An overview of vehicle dynamics How to tune handling for differing applications Guidance for selecting aftermarket components, including anti-roll bars, springs, shocks, bushings, chassis braces, camber adjusters, wheels, and brakes Tire and wheel selection advice Case-study projects Whether you're building a high-performance street car, an autocrosser, or a track-day machine, High-Performance Handling for Street or Track will help you create an integrated suspension system and tune it for maximum performance"-- Provided by publisher.
ISBN 978-0-7603-3994-7 (pbk.)
1. Automobiles--Handling characteristics. 2. Automobiles--Performance. 3. Hot rods--Design and construction. I.
Title.
TL245.5.A44 2011
629.2'31--dc22
                                    2011003751

Editors: Jeffrey Zuehlke, Jordan Wiklund
Design Manager: Kim Winscher
Cover Design: Simon Larkin
Layout: Heather Parlato

Printed in China

**On the cover:** Porsche 911. *Transtock*

**Cover insets:**
Adjustable coilcover shocks by *Progress Technology*
Aftermarket wheels by *Progress Technology*
Porsche 911 GT2. *Hotchkis Sport Suspension*

**On the back cover:** '68 Roadrunner. *Hotchkis Sport Suspension*

# Contents

# Acknowledgments

In 1969, my engineering school buddy and default driving coach, Kim Beno, was an intern at *Road & Track* magazine. We knew Ron Wakefield, the engineering editor at the time. We were trying to figure out how to make my 1957 Alfa Romeo Guilietta handle better since I just received my SCCA Novice Permit. We met with Ron, who told us to use bigger antiroll bars and allow for some adjustment to the rear bar in order to balance the handling. We followed Ron's advice and, guess what? It worked. And I was hooked! This started me on the career path that has led to this book. I haven't seen Ron Wakefield in 40 years, but despite his getting me involved in this crazy engineering endeavor, Kim and I are still close friends. Thanks to both of them for their help and friendship.

There are many others who have helped along the way. Thanks to each of you. In particular:

Bob Eckhardt, a racing friend with whom I've shared many adventures

Jeff Cheechov from Progress Technology, the best engineer and crew chief I've worked with. We worked together on many projects that reached 1 g cornering when that was unheard of for a street vehicle.

Paul VanValkenberg
Smokey Yunick
Steve Smith, Steve Smith Autosports
John Hotchkis, Hotchkis Sport Tuning
Wilfred Eibach, Eibach Springs
Gary Peek, Eibach Springs
Jonathan Spiegel
Bill Bainbridge, Hankook Tires
Jay Jones, TMC/Toyo Tires
Earl Knoper
Shari Arfons-McCullough, McCullough PR
Rick Brennen, Kumho Tires
John Rastetter, Tire Rack
Greg Woo
Bill Neumann, Neuspeed
Mark Richter, Falken Tires
Bob Bondurant
Danny McKeever, The Driver's Connection
Dave Royce, National Autosport Association
Ryan Flaherty, National Autosport Association

# Introduction

Flash back twenty years to when the first version of this book hit the stores. Computers were just starting to be used for designing suspension geometry. The learning curve was very steep and the Internet was not a factor. Today we rely on computers for design work—which is mostly good—and nearly everyone looks for answers on the Internet—which mostly isn't good! When I started in motorsports over 50 years ago, life was simple. We barely knew how to adjust tire pressures. The bar has been raised considerably since then. Information is everywhere. Back then, finding out how to make a car handle better was the challenge. Little information was available. Several people broke ground by publishing solid, engineering-based info. I have been lucky enough to work with several of these people and count them as friends. Carroll Smith led the way for road racers and Steve Smith was on the forefront for the oval track crowd. Possibly the most significant was Paul VanValkenburg. And then there was the legendary Smokey Yunick, the ultimate character but possibly the smartest guy I ever worked with. What each of the guys had in common was an engineering-based background combined with hands-on, real world experience. They had no hidden agenda. They honestly tried to help racers go faster, especially when their careers morphed from competition to writing. If you listened to what they said, and worked harder than anyone else applying that knowledge, you had a distinct advantage: knowledge—the Unfair Advantage!

Today, top teams, even at the amateur level of motorsports, employ engineers. The knowledge base is huge. Analyzing data is a big job. The one thing that has been consistent, however, is that the winner's circle is still occupied by those who work the hardest and the smartest. The winners are the ones who have taken the time to understand the basics of vehicle dynamics, car setup, and driving skills. And they work hard applying that understanding in the effort to reach the finish line first.

Meanwhile, everyone else looks for the magic bullet! When I first started racing formula cars in the 1960s, everyone was trying to figure out what the best spring rate was for your Formula Ford. No one knew about motion ratios and suspension frequencies. But some of us learned by studying and through trial and error. Others tried to copy what the fast guys were doing—the newest tire or gadget was always the "must have" answer. But that rarely worked and brought little success. Yet that methodology (or lack thereof) remains today. But it's even more rampant with the Internet and huge amounts of information presented by "experts" on forums and web articles. It has made finding the "TRUTH" even more difficult. I can offer one insight. I have never read comments in a forum or chat room about suspension, vehicle dynamics, or setup that is even in the ballpark. Information from these so-called experts ranges from useless to dangerous.

Yes, some articles on the web and in magazines are good, but most are rubbish. How do you know what's good or bad? Tough question! But the laws of physics do not change! (If they do we have bigger issues than making our car handle better!) And lap times don't lie. There's a good chance that since you're reading this book, you have a distinct advantage over those who are asking you what your setup is or what spring rate you're using! But if you want to improve, seek knowledge and trust your instincts about its validity and the worth of the information you find. Apply it with caution. Don't be afraid to ask questions from your fellow enthusiasts. They probably don't know any more than you do, but the fastest guys are often willing to share knowledge. I've had fellow competitors ask why I am willing to honestly give information. There are two answers: 1) Many others have done the same for me over the years, and 2) the best place to hide something valuable is in plain sight!

Finally and most importantly, always look at the entire system. Many racers make the mistake of looking in one or two areas for solutions, usually because they understand those areas better. But the system is complex. The final answer is always where the action is—where the tire meets the track. Optimizing car handling for the street is challenging; for the track it is a daunting endeavor. But taking on the challenge and mastering this art and science is exceptionally rewarding and, I suppose, the reason I've been doing it for more than 50 years. I used to tell people that "this ain't rocket science!" Turns out I was wrong! But it is supposed to be fun. And some how, the harder you work and the more you learn, the more fun it is!

—Don Alexander

# Chapter 1
# What Is Handling?

**Y**ou just purchased a new Honda Civic and you've decided to improve performance with a suspension package, wheels, and tires. You want to improve performance and the look of the car. You find an online parts seller, order a suspension package, plus-size wheels, and a set of ultra high performance tires. You and a buddy install the package without too much difficulty, get the tires mounted, and you're ready to go. You have high expectations for your new "ride." It looks great with the two-inch lowering springs and you expect it to stick like glue around your favorite interstate ramps. You and your friend go out for a test drive.

## ON THE STREET

Before you installed the package, you "tested" the handling on the interstate ramps and some canyon roads. The car felt a little mushy, didn't have much grip from the OE tires but had a comfortable ride over the ruts and bumps from the deteriorating road surfaces. It was fun to drive in spite of the excessive "lean," or body roll.

Now you expect the modifications to transform your ride into a canyon carver—not quite a race car, but definitely faster and way more fun to drive. The first thing you notice is the scraping when you pull into your friend's driveway. The lowered suspension means you must be careful when entering and exiting driveways and going over drainage channels, ruts, and bumps. After a couple of blocks, you hit a pothole, one that wasn't too noticeable with the stock suspension. This time, it nearly knocks your teeth out. But you figure it's a small price to pay for the improved handling.

Handling is best defined on the track, where you can safely drive to the limits of the tires' adhesion.

Drifting creates a unique set of compromises. What would be considered good handling for a drift car would be terrible for a track car or on the highway.

Some cars, like this Lotus, offer exceptional handling without modifications.

You get to the interstate entry ramp, entering the turn-in at about five miles per hour faster than normal. The front end turns in very quickly and you can feel the new ultra high performance tires grab the road surface. There's nearly no body roll. The car feels just the way you had hoped. Compared to the stock setup, the modifications make the car feel like a race car. You are very pleased and your confidence grows as you pick up the throttle and increase cornering speed as you round the 270-degree cloverleaf turn. As you reach the exit of the corner, you begin to accelerate hard, entering the interstate at speed with ease. You glance at your friend, and you're both smiling. Too cool! You are sure you have gone at least 10 miles per hour faster around the cloverleaf. What an improvement!

As you approach your favorite off-ramp, you decide to carry more speed into the s-series of turns, right then left, before the traffic signal at the end of the ramp. The car turns in crisply. You know you're near the limit as the tires are squealing loudly. You hit a small bump, one you never even noticed before, on the outside of the corner. The front tire glides over it, but when the rear tire hits, you feel a jolt and the rear of the car starts to slide out abruptly, totally surprising you. But you react by countersteering and lifting off the throttle. The car straightens out quickly, you avoid the guardrail on the outside of the corner, but the adrenaline rush sends your heart rate soaring. What the hell happened?

Other cars like this VW Beetle require extensive modifications.

Time attack cars offer tremendous latitude for suspension modification, making for very exciting competition. *Progress Technology*

Street legal drag racing requires good handling characteristics, especially for the launch, to optimize drive tire traction. *Progress Technology*

Often overlooked amidst all the technical and mechanical factors is the driver—who of course has a huge influence on "good handling."

Autocrossing, known as Solo II in the Sports Car Club of America, is an easy and inexpensive way to test your car's handling with virtually no risk. *Hotchkis Sport Suspension*

Even Bonneville requires good handling. Bonneville can be bumpy, but an absolute minimum amount of tire drag is crucial for top speed. *Progress Technology*

Tire traction is the key to good handling. The suspension is there to make sure all of the tire contact patches are working as much as possible.

If you hadn't pushed the car so close to the limit, you wouldn't have noticed the extreme oversteer, or loose handling condition. Most drivers never get close to the limits of traction, so handling problems are never really experienced. "Good" handling for one driver is not even in the ballpark for another driver. But just what happened in the above scenario?

The abrupt oversteer experienced in the above example is fairly common from aftermarket suspension manufacturer packages. Most packages are not properly engineered and tested. Several possibilities could have caused the oversteer. Most likely, the rear shocks had too little bump travel when compressing over the bump on the exit ramp. This caused the shock to bottom out, rapidly increasing the load on that tire, and causing a nearly instantaneous handling problem. If the shocks were included in the package, they were not properly specified for the application, being too short for adequate travel, providing too little bump travel before bottoming, not having a bump stop to slow travel before bottoming, or just being way too stiff in bump, or compression. If you're starting to get the picture that it takes a lot of engineering and testing to create a good suspension package, you are absolutely correct. Every component must work with every other component, or the package will leave a lot to be desired, or in some cases be downright dangerous.

## ON THE TRACK

Let's continue the opening story. You've been itching to try your car on the racetrack. You hear about a local group putting on a track day event at a track about 100 miles away.

You decide to give it try. All you need is a helmet. You make it through the safety inspection and the driver orientation, then head out with an instructor for an orientation lap. You can't wait to hit the track in your car.

You make it through the first session, realizing that you can go much faster. In the second session you pick up the pace. By the third session, you begin to feel pretty confident. By the fourth and last session of the day, you're getting close to the traction limit of the tires. As you push harder, you can feel the front tires beginning to slide a little. You have to crank in more steering lock to make it through some of the turns. This becomes worse as you push even harder. The car is trying to slide off the track. All you can do is slow down to keep the front of the car pointed into the turn. What felt great on the canyons and ramps and earlier when you were getting up to speed now feels sluggish, like an anchor is tied to the front of the car. The understeer, when the front tires lose traction before the rear, is significant. And it is wearing the front tires out at an alarming rate. Understeer is common on nearly all cars because it is stable and easier to recover from than oversteer, which occurs when the rear tires lose traction first, causing the car to try to spin out. So what caused the car to understeer so much?

Most auto manufacturers build understeer into the suspension because it is safer. Aftermarket suspension manufacturers often build understeer into packages as well, often for the same reasons. But most aftermarket companies try to reduce understeer to a bare minimum, the preferred setup for superior handling. Only a few companies have the expertise to actually achieve this goal.

Good tires are mandatory to achieve the best possible handling for street or track. This "R" compound tire is designed for track use; it is very soft and will wear very quickly on the highway. *Toyo Tire USA*

This ultra high performance tire from Toyo is excellent for highway use if you want great handling performance and good wear. It can also be used for limited track day and autocross use. *Toyo Tire USA*

Anti-roll bars can usually be purchased separately. They not only control body roll but also influence handling balance. *Progress Technology*

Understeer can be caused by several factors, ranging from front springs that are too stiff; rear anti-roll bars that are too soft; binding in the front suspension; incorrect camber angles on the tires; or incorrect tire pressures. It takes considerable work and experience to create a vehicle with "good handling" characteristics.

## SO WHAT IS GOOD HANDLING?

For many drivers, good handling is a feeling. Many drivers consider improved responsiveness to be improved handling. While that is part of the equation, for the performance car enthusiast, good handling encompasses much more than just feel. Good handling means improved cornering, braking, and acceleration performance, and getting the most from the four tire contact patches linking the car to the road. More traction during braking, cornering, and acceleration, quicker response to driver control inputs, good balance at the limit, and lower ETs or faster lap times are all big factors in the performance equation for improved handling.

Three factors create good handling. The first factor is making the best possible use of the tire's traction capacity. The second factor requires a good balance of traction front to rear. And the third factor means that the car is instantly responsive to the driver's steering, brake, and throttle inputs. Ride comfort is a consideration, but only a secondary one when maximum handling performance is being sought.

Maximum traction implies sticky tires. While sticky tires provide more traction, the bigger consideration is getting each of the four tire contact patches working as well as possible on the road surface. This combines the tire sidewall stiffness; suspension geometry; the ability of the springs and shocks to control the tires over bumps; the degree of roll resistance offered by the anti-roll bars and springs; and the compliance of the suspension bushings. While stickier tires may make your car corner, brake, and accelerate faster, you are losing handling performance if those four little tire contact patches are not hooked up to the road.

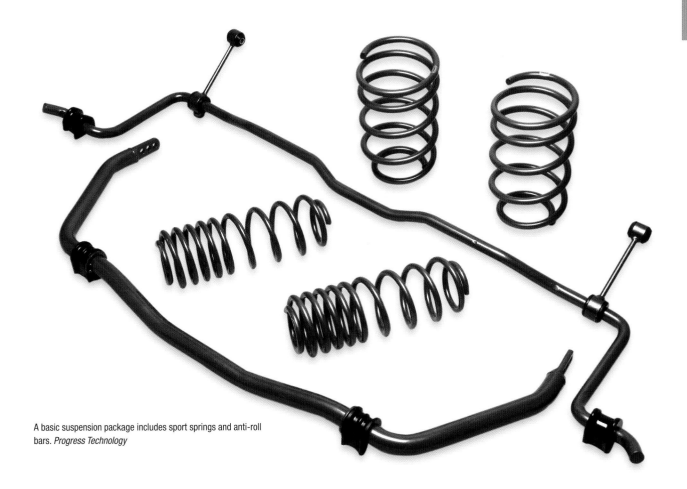

A basic suspension package includes sport springs and anti-roll bars. *Progress Technology*

The second factor is handling balance. Most everyone has heard the term "push" or "loose" in TV coverage of races. A push, or understeer, as noted above, means the front tires lose traction before the rear. The car will not turn as much as it should as the limits of tire traction are reached. Ultimately, the car will continue straight ahead even when the steering wheel is turned to full lock. A loose condition, or oversteer, means the rear tires lose traction before the front tires. The car will turn more than it should as the tires reach the limits of traction. As the car oversteers, the driver must apply opposite steering lock to keep the car pointed in the desired direction. At the extreme, the car will spin. The biggest influence on handling balance, that point where the car does not understeer or oversteer (it's neutral) is the balance of roll resistance between the front springs and anti-roll bar vs. the rear springs and anti-roll bar. If a car is neutral

handling and the rear anti-roll bar or springs are made stiffer, the car will become loose, or oversteer. If the front springs or bars are made stiffer, the car will push, or understeer. The job of the aftermarket spring and anti-roll manufacturers is to control body roll and create the optimum balance between front and rear roll resistance so that the handling balance is near neutral.

Many factors contribute to "good handling." A well-conceived suspension system addresses all of these factors and utilizes suspension components that are compatible for the car, the driving/road conditions, and the degree of desired handling performance. Ill-conceived systems can hurt cornering performance, provide less than "good handling" and deteriorate ride quality as well. In the next chapter we'll take a look at the factors and components that must be right to achieve good handling.

Adjustable anti-roll bars allow fine tuning of handling balance. *Progress Technology*

Adjustable coilover shocks allow fine tuning of ride heights and allow adjustment of corner weights. *Progress Technology*

# Chapter 2
# Factors Affecting Vehicle Handling Performance

**B**y now, it's becoming clear that many elements must be considered in both the design process as well as the selection process. When a company sets out to design and build a suspension system for a given vehicle, the factors they should consider are many. Not all suspension companies take this approach, however. And for you to make the best possible decision about the right package for your car and use, you need to have a basic understanding of these factors. Here is a brief look at them.

## TIRE LOADS

When a car is at rest, a certain amount of weight rests on each tire contact patch. This static weight distribution is a factor in determining the traction at each corner of the car. The traction of a tire is proportional to the weight, or load, on the tire contact patch. If the load increases, the traction increases; if the load decreases, the traction decreases. However, the relationship is non-linear, meaning that if the load is doubled on a tire, the traction is something less than double. We'll look at this in more detail in the next chapter.

The key to optimum handling and maximum traction is balancing tire load on all four tire contact patches.

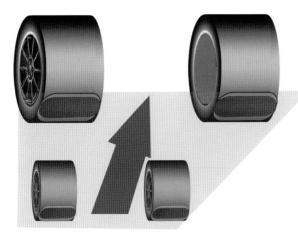

The key to optimum handling and maximum traction is balancing tire load on all four tire contact patches.

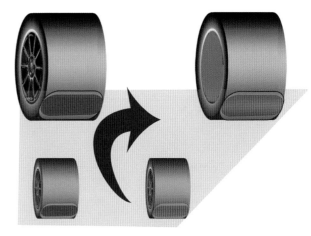

During steady state cornering, weight transfers from the inside to the outside tires. This reduces overall traction, and the amount of weight transfer at the front vs. the rear affects handling balance.

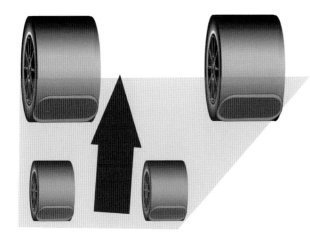

While braking, weight transfers from the rear to the front tires.

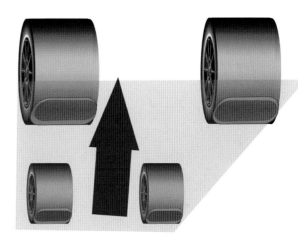

During acceleration, weight transfers from the front tires to the rear.

## WEIGHT TRANSFER

When a car accelerates, brakes, or corners, some portion of the weight will shift from front to rear, rear to front, or inside to outside. This changes the traction at each tire contact patch. For a given car and rate of acceleration, slowing, or cornering, a given amount of weight will transfer from one set of tires (front, rear, left or right) to the opposite set of tires. In addition, there are three factors of weight transfer affecting handling: where the weight is transferred, how fast it gets there, and when it is transferred.

Weight moves from the front to the rear under acceleration, from the rear to the front under braking, and from the inside to the outside while cornering. But while cornering, some of the weight moves to the front outside and some moves to the rear outside. The stiffness of the springs and anti-roll bars (roll resistance) determines how much moves to the outside front vs. the outside rear. If a spring or anti-roll bar is stiffer at one end of the car, that end of the car will get more of the sideways weight transfer during cornering. That end of the car will also have less traction relative to the other end of the car. For example, stiffening the front springs or anti-roll bars will cause more weight to transfer to the outside front and cause more understeer or push (or reduce oversteer). Anti-roll bars and springs rates are used to control this handling balance.

**17**

Compliance in the suspension system determines how quickly weight is transferred. Suspension bushings are a small factor here, but the major control over how fast weight moves is the shock absorber. Stiffer shocks cause weight to move faster. Softer shocks cause weight to move slower. Stiffer shocks (combined with stiffer springs) reduce ride comfort. Shocks that are too stiff can cause poor tire contact patch compliance over bumpy road surfaces as well as causing the car to be too responsive. Again, the shocks must be part of an integrated suspension system designed for a specific application and set of conditions.

When weight transfer occurs is based on when the driver uses the controls and how quickly those controls are moved. Abrupt use of the controls can cause abrupt weight transfer and deteriorate the quality of handling and upset the handling balance. We will discuss this subject a bit more in the next chapter.

## TIRE PRESSURE

Tire pressures affect the shape of the tire contact patch, which affects the load across the tread of the tire. If a tire is overinflated, the center of the contact patch is loaded more than the edges of the contact patch. Underinflation has the opposite effect. Finding the optimum tire pressure for the car, tires, wheels, and suspension system assures that each contact patch is evenly loaded and maximum traction is available.

Springs affect where weight is transferred while the shock absorber influences how quickly weight is transferred.

The driver influences handling through when and how fast the steering wheel turning is turned. *Hotchkis Sport Suspension*

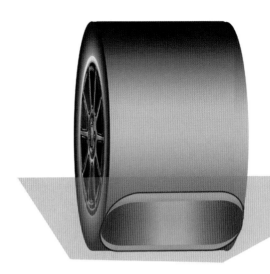

While the load on each tire contact patch is a major factor in good handling and total traction, so is the load distribution at the tire contact patch. Here the load is too low at the center of the tire because the tire pressure is too low.

Here the tire pressure is too high.

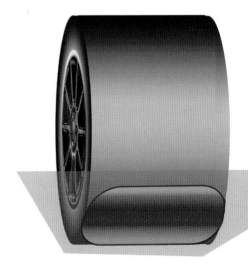

In this illustration, the tire pressure is correct.

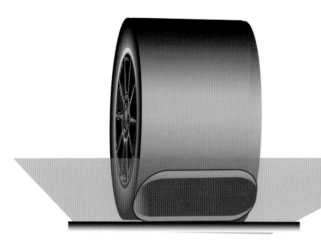

The camber angle, or tilt of the tire when viewed from the front, must be correct for optimum loading on the tire contact patch, as shown here.

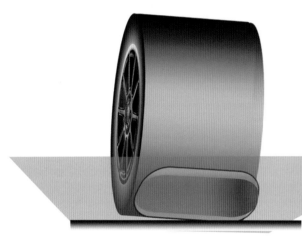

Here there is too much negative camber.

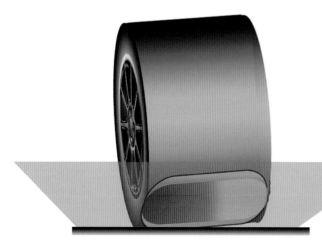

Too little negative camber puts too much load on the outside part of the tire contact patch.

## CAMBER

Camber is the tilt of a tire when viewed from the front. Camber is positive if the top of the tire is tilted to the outside and negative if the tilt is to the inside. Since most suspension systems gain positive camber during bump (compression) travel, and the outside tire goes into bump during cornering, some amount of negative camber is needed to offset the camber gain and keep the tire contact patch flat on the road surface during cornering.

## CAMBER GAIN

Camber gain is determined by suspension geometry. During body roll, it's usually the outside front tire that gains camber. This tilts the tire contact patch and changes the loading across the tread and reduces traction. Some static negative camber can compensate for this, but too much negative camber causes accelerated tire wear and hurts straight line braking performance. Stiffer front spring and anti-roll bars reduce body roll, which reduces bump travel and camber gain. This reduces the amount of static negative camber needed to keep the tire contact patch flat on the road surface in a corner.

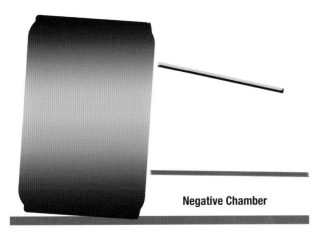

**Negative Chamber**

Negative camber is present when the top of the tire is tilted toward the inside of the car.

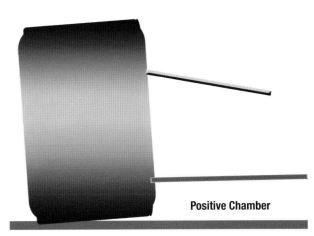

**Positive Chamber**

Positive camber is present when the top of the tire is tilted toward the outside of the car.

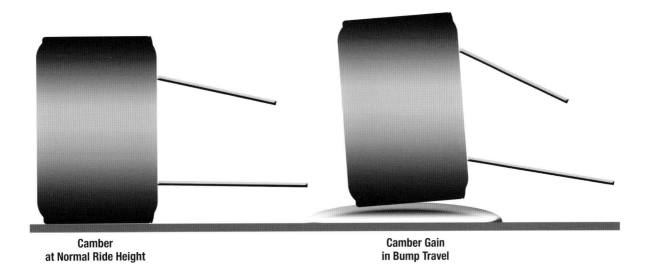

**Camber
at Normal Ride Height**

**Camber Gain
in Bump Travel**

Camber gain is caused by the suspension geometry, causing a change in camber angle when body roll occurs. Limiting body roll reduces this effect.

## TOE

Toe is the angle of the front tires when viewed from above. Toe-in means the fronts of the tires are closer together than the rears of the tires. Toe-out is the opposite. Cars will turn into a corner better with a small amount of toe-out. Toe-in offers more stability in a straight line, so for daily highway and street driving, a small amount of toe-in is preferred. Too much toe-in or toe-out will increase tire wear. Rear suspensions can also have toe-in or toe-out. Some cars actually work better with a small amount of toe-out at the rear, but most cars need some toe-in at the rear to assure straight-line stability, especially for drag racing or high-speed road courses.

## CASTER

Caster is the angle of the steering axis at the front of the car when viewed from the side (see illustration). More caster increases the self-centering effect of the steering, but also increases tire scrub slightly while cornering. Different caster angles on the left and right side cause the steering to pull in one direction. Using the factory recommended caster angle is preferred.

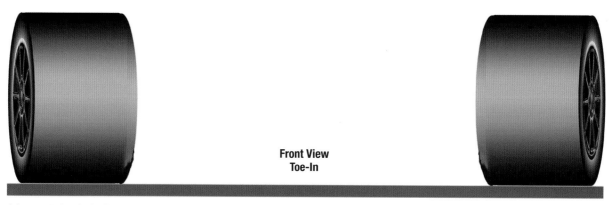

**Front View**
**Toe-In**

Toe-in is present when the leading edge of the tires at one end of the car are angled toward the car's centerline.

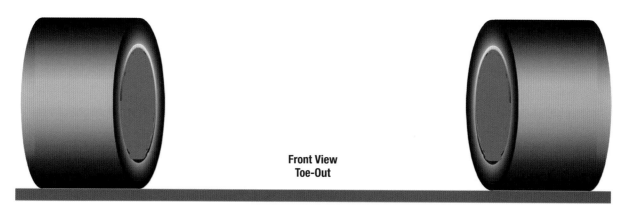

**Front View**
**Toe-Out**

Toe-out is present when the leading edge of the tires at one end of the car are angled away from the car's centerline.

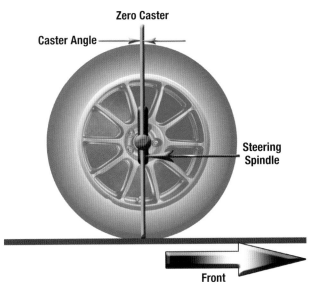

Caster is the tilt of the steering axis when viewed from the side of the car. Zero caster, as shown here, is when the axis is perfectly vertical.

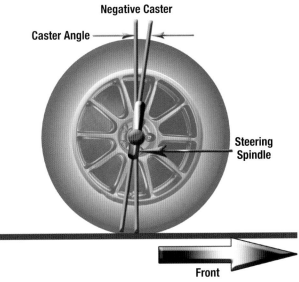

Negative caster is present when the steering axis is tilted toward the front.

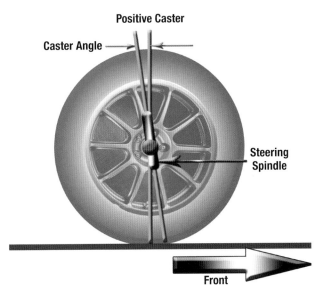

Positive caster is present when the steering axis is tilted toward the rear.

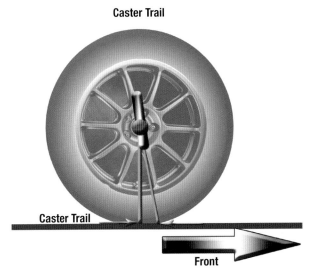

Caster trail is the measurement on the ground between the vertical line through the center of the wheel and the a-line running through the steering axis.

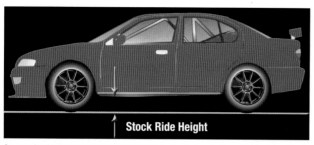

**Stock Ride Height**

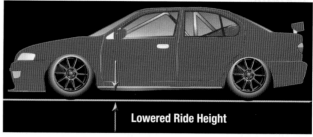

**Lowered Ride Height**

Suspension kits are usually used to lower the car, as seen in these illustrations. The lower the car, the lower the center of gravity; that means less weight transfer. But making the car too low reduces wheel travel and leads to the chassis and body bottoming out, which causes serious handing problems.

## RIDE HEIGHT

Lowering a car reduces weight transfer and improves cornering performance by lowering the center of gravity. It also reduces suspension travel, so stiffer springs are needed to keep the car from bottoming out over bumps or bottoming on the suspension, which can cause damage, especially to shock absorbers.

## SPRINGS

The job of the springs is first to keep the car from bottoming, second to allow the tire contact patches to stay on the road surface over bumps, and finally to partially control body roll. Stiffer springs allow a car to have a lower ride height and also reduce body roll; both are important for improved handling. On the other side, stiffer springs reduce the ability of the tire contact patch to stay on the road surface over bumps, hurting traction over bumps as well as increasing ride harshness. Springs must be designed to be a compromise for a given set of conditions.

## ANTI-ROLL BARS

Anti-roll bars serve two purposes. First, they are intended to control body roll so that camber gain is not excessive. Second, the bars are a convenient way to balance the roll resistance front to rear to achieve the best handling balance. Both of these can be affected with springs, but to really control body roll with springs would require springs too stiff for either ride comfort or control over bumpy roads.

## SHOCKS

Shocks are designed to control spring movements over bumps. Without shocks, the springs would continue to oscillate, causing the car to wallow down the road. In a performance application, shocks are used to control how fast weight is transferred and thus influence the responsiveness of the car to driver control inputs. Shocks can be tuned in both bump and rebound travel and at a variety of shaft speeds to achieve a variety of handling characteristics under many varying road or track conditions. Shocks must be designed to work in a specific application to achieve good handling characteristics.

Shown here are a coilover spring, shock absorber, and an adjusting collar for a coilover suspension. *Progress Technology*

Anti-roll bars reduce body roll (but not weight transfer) and are used to manipulate where weight is transferred front to rear, which affects handling balance. *Progress Technology*

## BUSHINGS

Suspension bushings are intended to isolate road noise and vibration from the car occupants. Stock bushings are usually made of rubber. The soft rubber insulates well but also allows a high degree of compliance in the suspension. This kills responsiveness to driver control inputs and increases suspension deflection, hurting overall handling performance. Solid metal bushings reduce compliance to nearly zero, but are noisy and harsh. Urethane bushings reduce compliance considerably, but maintain some comfort and noise control. Just adding performance bushings to your car will improve handling noticeably.

## CHASSIS BRACING

A variety of chassis stiffeners and strut tower braces are available for many street and motorsports applications. By reducing chassis flex, the suspension moves less, making the car more responsive and reducing handling issues like camber change.

When a chassis flexes, it acts like an undamped spring, which can be very difficult to control and tune. Chassis bracing improves handling but also makes the ride more harsh.

## TUNING

Even after installing a fully integrated suspension system consisting of springs, anti-roll bars, shocks, bushings, wheels, and tires, the system needs to be tuned for optimum performance. At a minimum, the proper tire pressures and suspension alignment settings must be found. Tuning can make big improvements in handling performance once you have the best components on your car. The scope of tuning your suspension is broad and a major part of this book is devoted to alignment and tuning. Even for the street, tuning pays significant dividends in improved performance and better tire wear. And the best handling car is also the safest, since good handling and braking means you have a better chance to avoid an accident.

Suspension bushings locate suspension pivot points and can be an issue when compliance is too great. Stock bushings are usually soft, causing compliance and reduced precision and control. Urethane bushings offer a good compromise for the street, reducing compliance but maintaining some comfort and reduced noise over solid metal bushings. The bushings used in the Hotchkis a-arm are stiffer urethane bushings. *Hotchkis Sport Suspension*

While well-engineered parts are a key starting point for improved handling, tuning the suspension to optimize tire traction is imperative. Here Jeff Cheechov from Progress Technology takes tire temperatures on an Acura after a skid pad run.

FACTORS AFFECTING VEHICLE HANDLING PERFORMANCE

# FRONT DRIVE, REAR DRIVE, AND ALL-WHEEL DRIVE

While each type of drive system has its quirks, the tire contact patches do not know what type of drive system they are trying to control. The tire contact patches only know how much load is resting on each of them, and how that load changes dynamically as the car accelerates, brakes, and corners. Generally we do the same things to a front drive that we do to a rear or all-wheel drive vehicle to get the handling balanced and maximum traction from the entire vehicle. The differences are more in weight distribution and the work load of the drive wheels than in the drive system itself. There are a few exceptions.

First, the higher suspension frequency (determined by spring rate among other factors—see the Wheel Rates and Suspension Frequencies section of Chapter 3) will go at the driven end of the vehicle with an all-wheel drive being treated as a front drive if the weight bias is to the front. Second, on a front drive vehicle with more than about 59 percent of the weight on the front end, the rear roll stiffness should be high enough to unweight the inside rear tire contact patch considerably in a corner, even lifting off the road surface. The other way to achieve the desired results is to use narrower tires on the rear than on the front. This is done to balance the workload of the front and rear tires in order to achieve a neutral handling balance. This is usually what is needed to counteract understeer, and is usually done with a stiffer anti-roll bar. On the highway, a slightly softer setup is needed for stability. Beyond these specifics, we engineer and tune the chassis in exactly the same way regardless of the drive system. Having said that, the driver will need to take a different approach when driving a front drive platform versus a rear or all-wheel drive chassis.

Rear-drive cars have a distinct advantage since weight transfers to the rear under acceleration. This improves traction for acceleration, but a good limited slip differential is needed to drive both rear tires.

All-wheel drive has a great advantage since all four wheels accelerate the car exiting a corner. This advantage becomes even greater when conditions get slippery, like rain, snow, or dirt; this is why most rally cars are AWD. *Eibach Springs*

Front-wheel drive has a distinct disadvantage since weight transfer during acceleration is off of the drive wheels. Front-drive is less of an issue with low power and faster corners. It is at its worst on low speed corners as found in autocrossing.

26

For many older cars, the ultimate way
to improve suspension geometry is to replace
the entire sub-frame. The 1967–1969 Camaro front sub-frame
from Hotchkis improves geometry and works well with modern tires.
*Hotchkis Sport Suspension*

This custom upper a-arm from Hotchkis is much stronger and uses stiff bushings
to reduce compliance. *Hotchkis Sport Suspension*

Engine bay stiffeners can reduce chassis flex. This Camaro kit from Hotchkis includes an engine bay stiffener made from tubing. *Hotchkis Sport Suspension*

This is an engine bay stiffener from Hotchkis installed on a Camaro. *Hotchkis Sport Suspension*

## THE ISSUES

There are two major factors to consider before you begin the quest for improved handling. First, how will the car be used?

- Street or highway only
- Combination of highway and motorsports
- Competition only

Second, what compromises must you make, or are you willing to make, to achieve improved handling? These will be different for each individual and for each of the above categories. Are you willing to tolerate a very bumpy ride, one that can make the car very skittish on the highway, to improve performance on a smoother surface, like a racetrack or an autocross course in a smooth parking lot? Or are you willing to sacrifice some ultimate cornering performance to make your vehicle more forgiving and comfortable on the road? A goal of this book is to help you make those decisions and end up with the best performance package for your use and budget.

### For Street and Highway Only

Consider these factors:

- Type of daily driving
- Fun driving (mountain roads, canyons, interstate ramps)
- Budget
- Importance of ride quality
- Ground clearance
- Appearance
- Product availability for your vehicle
- Driving skills
- Mechanical skills

### Combined Street and Motorsports

If you plan to compete with your daily driver, consider these factors:

- Type of event (drag race, autocross, rally, track days)
- Category of competition
- Rules
- Budget
- Product availability for your vehicle
- Ease of conversion (tires/wheels, ride height, alignment)
- Ride quality
- Ground clearance

### Competition Only

This one is much easier. The compromises are simply to make your vehicle as fast as possible. But you should still consider the following:

- Type of competition
- Suitability of your vehicle
- Class
- Budget
- Availability of parts for your vehicle
- Mechanical skills
- Driving skills

This unique anti-roll bar from Hotchkis is used on older cars not originally equipped with rear anti-roll bars. *Hotchkis Sport Suspension*

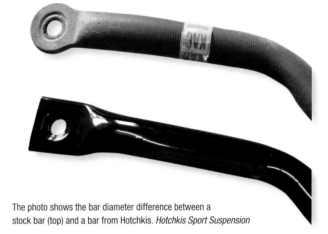

The photo shows the bar diameter difference between a stock bar (top) and a bar from Hotchkis. *Hotchkis Sport Suspension*

Keep in mind that going to extremes for pure performance may cause you considerable grief. A suspension system that is extremely stiff may be faster for some cars, but may make your car slower. Consider the track surface condition and your own driving skills. If you get many hours of "seat time" each season, you can get away with a stiffer setup. But if you are new to track driving, a softer, more conservative setup will actually allow you to drive closer to the limit and really feel what the car is doing under you. If the setup is too stiff, events may occur too quickly for you to be able sense and keep up with them.

But in the end, your goals and desires, along with your budget, will make most of your decisions for you. The rest is simply the compromises you must make to achieve your goal. And that includes selecting a company that really knows how to design and build a system for your type of vehicle. We will look more closely at those issues in greater detail throughout this book.

# Chapter 3
# What Is Vehicle Dynamics?

**B**efore we delve into the somewhat complex topic of vehicle dynamics, let's look at some interesting changes in the world of performance handling in the last decade. Many of these changes have to do with information, or more accurately, misinformation due in large part to the Internet.

A couple of years ago, I was invited to co-drive a Honda Challenge car in an endurance race at Buttonwillow Raceway Park in California. The car was fairly competitive in its class, but the owner/driver was not very experienced. While this story is more pertinent for track cars and driving, the point relates nearly as well to street vehicles as much as track and multi-use cars.

On my first lap of practice, I was quite surprised at how stiffly suspended the car was. It was horrible over bumpy sections and difficult to drive quickly. Since the track is bumpy in places, there was no advantage to a stiff setup; in fact, it was a major disadvantage. While I had the experience to compensate for the stiff suspension over the bumps, my co-driver did not, and that made him slower in the car than he needed to be.

The car had stiff springs and very stiff shocks, causing the car to react very quickly to driver steering inputs. A driver with highly developed skills can use this to their advantage on a smooth track, but with a less experienced driver, the stiff setup makes it very difficult to feel the tires as the limit of traction is approached. That makes it easy to overdrive the corners, causing increased overheating of the tires and tire wear. Or, because the car feels very "twitchy," the driver stays well below the traction limit, not negotiating the corners with maximum speed. Ironically, both situations cause valuable time to be lost. The "sweet spot" is somewhere in between, and with a stiff suspension, the sweet spot is very small, kind of like trying to hit a hard serve with an old, small-framed tennis racket compared to a modern, oversized racket. The softer suspension setup has a larger sweet spot, making finding the limit easier and far more precise.

One of the issues with an ultra stiff setup is driver fatigue, which is a concern in an endurance race. The driver must use more attention for driving the car, with less attention available

A skid pad is much like a dynometer for the tires and suspension. Only a handful of suspension companies use a skid pad, or any other track, for testing and tuning. *Progress Technology*

for strategy and tactics. And the rough ride just beats on the driver, adding to the fatigue.

After my practice session, I saw the crew chief first. He happened to be the owner of the company that built the suspension for this Honda, and an old friend, one who knows better than to use an ultra stiff suspension on this track, especially with a newer driver. I asked him what the deal was. He said that the owner/driver of the Honda insisted on this setup, which had been recommended by the Honda Challenge champion in a similar car. The champion had been racing for several years, and was on track about 30 weekends a season—in other words both very experienced, but also highly skilled with very fast reflexes. Even after explaining the issues to the owner/driver of the car, he was adamant about sticking with the setup, which he did for at least a couple of years.

After the event, he e-mailed me a link to a Honda Challenge tech forum thread about spring rates for Honda Challenge cars. I read all of the entries and discussions. Not one person on the thread had a clue about determining the optimum spring rate for a car. Most of the

discussion was about "so-and-so runs 500-pound front spring in his World Challenge car." Or, "this guy uses a 400 front spring in his Civic Honda Challenge car at track XYZ."

Nowhere in the forum discussion thread did anyone even mention wheel rate or suspension frequency, a sure sign of a lack of knowledge and understanding. (A little later in this chapter we will discuss wheel rates of springs and suspension frequencies, two crucial factors relevant to selecting the optimum spring for a specific use, be it highway or racetrack, and even for a specific track and tire combination.) When you are deciding on a suspension system for your car, regardless of the purpose and use, it is important to have a basic understanding of all of the important factors, at least enough to know that if the company building a suspension system doesn't understand these factors, and address them in the design procedure, steer clear of them and spend your hard-earned bucks with someone who puts in as much work on the suspension system as you do earning the money to buy it. And believe me when I tell you, many companies do not have clue about the factors affecting suspension design.

31

The Banks Sidewinder, a Dodge Dakota pickup with a Cummins turbo diesel engine, was extensively modified for Bonneville. With nearly 800 horsepower and 1,400 pound-feet of torque, the truck set land speed records for pickups at Bonneville at over 222 miles per hour with the author driving. He also designed the suspension for this street legal monster. Even with the massive Cummins engine up front, the Sidewinder handled quite well on the road.

## VEHICLE DYNAMICS EXPLAINED

Vehicle dynamics is, simply stated, the study of the forces that affect the performance of a car. The reality is that the car's systems, the forces acting on them, and the way those forces are controlled is very complex, and one that few engineers understand fully. But there are some basics that need to be understood in order to make sound decisions about handling performance. For improved handling performance on the street, a basic understanding will help you make sound decisions about the compromises you need to make to achieve you goals. For any form of competition, an understanding of dynamics is needed to find the maximum level of handling performance. Without this knowledge, you may occasionally get lucky with a setup, but the knowledge and how you apply it will allow you to find the optimum setup much more consistently.

For our purposes, we will focus on a competition setup, since it is easier to understand. For street performance, other parameters come into play, like ride comfort, tire wear, budget, and how the car will be used. For competition all we care about is getting the car around (or down) the racetrack as quickly as possible. And to bring this down to the simplest factor, all we really care about is maximum acceleration,

braking, and cornering force. And that means finding the most traction possible within the parameters we must work within. Whether it's for a single pass down a drag strip, one run on an autocross course, or a 12-hour endurance road race, we want to find the most possible traction for the required length of time.

It's fairly easy—or at least easier—to find maximum traction for acceleration without worrying about cornering or braking, but we must find the best compromise between the often-conflicting dynamics needs of cornering, braking, and accelerating. And the setup for max traction for a single lap or pass is much easier to find than the setup that allows the highest possible *average* traction over a long event. And finally, many competitors mistakenly look at the car system as a series of individual systems that are not connected to each other. In reality, the systems are related to each other and no single system can be ignored if true success is to be found.

The system almost always overlooked by nearly all competitors, especially drivers, is the driver. What a driver does with the controls, when they are used, how quickly they are used, and for how long, affects the dynamics of the overall car system and should always be considered in the overall picture. The driver has a dramatic effect on performance, and subtle changes in technique can often improve dynamic car performance.

Here are several considerations:

### Tire Slip Angle

The tire slip angle, which is actually the amount of twist in the tire sidewall that causes the tire contact patch to turn at a smaller angle than the wheel centerline (the difference is the slip angle) determines the lateral force of the tire. At a given slip angle, the tire will create the maximum cornering force. At a smaller slip angle, the tire will create less cornering force and the same holds true at greater slip angles. The goal for the driver is to keep the tire at the optimum slip angle for maximum cornering force at all times in a corner—not an easy task. The front tire slip angles vs. the rear tire slip angles determine the handling balance of the car. If they are equal, the car is neutral. If the fronts are bigger than the rears, the car will push or understeer. If the rears are greater, the car will be loose or oversteer.

### Total Weight

Lighter is better. For competition purposes, most classes have minimum weight rules. You want to be at minimum weight. If there is no minimum weight rule, run as light as you can. There are two big reasons that minimum weight is important. First, the engine must accelerate the extra weight. You have probably noticed that your street car does not accelerate as well with three passengers on board as it does with just you in the car. Second is the factor we looked at above—tire traction vs. vertical load on the tire. If you add 500 pounds to the car to improve handling, you have added 500 pounds to the tire's workload, but only about 450 pounds of additional traction force. That makes the car slower under braking and cornering. It's not a good tradeoff.

### Weight Transfer

As discussed in the previous chapter, during cornering, weight transfers from the inside to the outside; under braking, weight transfers from the rear to the front; under acceleration it transfers from the front to the rear. Weight transfer hurts overall vehicle traction. In cornering situations, weight moves off the inside tires to the outside tires. This changes vertical load on all four tires. Two tires (the inside) lose vertical load while the other two gain vertical load. The inside tires lose traction while the outside tires gain traction. Sounds okay so far. But remember that the relationship between vertical load on a tire and the traction force of that tire is *not* linear. The weight coming off the inside tires causes them to lose traction faster than the outside tires gain traction from the new-found additional vertical load. So the net total traction of the tires is reduced compared to the same situation if no weight transfer occurred. Since it is not possible to eliminate weight transfer in a corner, we at least want to minimize it so that the overall traction remains as high as possible.

Drivers review data logging with the team owner during a test for an endurance racer. Gale Banks is flanked by author on the right and Dave Royce on the left.

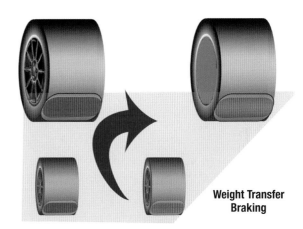

**Weight Transfer Braking**

Remember: the ultimate goal for maximum traction is to have equal load on all four tire contact patches.

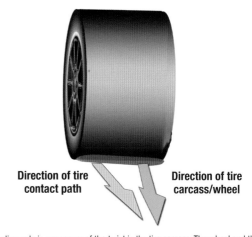

**Direction of tire contact path**

**Direction of tire carcass/wheel**

A tire's slip angle is a measure of the twist in the tire carcass. The wheel and the contact patch do not move in the same direction. The wheel turns more than the contact patch. The difference in angles is the slip angle. When front and rear slip angles are not identical, a handling imbalance exists. When the front slip angle is greater, the car is understeering at the limits of traction. If the front angle is less, the car is oversteering at the limits of traction.

Under braking, the same thing occurs, but is less pronounced. Under acceleration on a rear-drive car, weight transfer actually helps accelerate the car because the drive wheels are gaining traction while the tires losing traction are not driving the car. The opposite is true for a front drive car, which makes the elapsed times of the front drive import drag cars all the more impressive. Even though we gain some acceleration traction from more weight transfer, if you have to turn and slow down for corners, weight transfer hurts lap times, so our goal is to minimize weight transfer as much as possible.

There are only four factors that affect the amount of weight transferred.

- The total weight of the vehicle—more weight means more weight transfer, all else being equal
- The force acting on the center of gravity—more force means more weight transfer
- The height of the center of gravity above ground—higher centers of gravity transfer more weight
- The track width (for cornering) or the wheelbase (for acceleration and braking)—narrower track widths or shorter wheelbase means more weight transfer

### Nothing else affects the amount of weight transfer

Let's look a little more closely at each of these. Total weight we have already discussed. Since we want to run as light as possible, or at minimum weight, this is a constant factor which we cannot change unless we make major changes to the vehicle. The traction force of the tires determines the force acting at the center of gravity. Reducing the traction or driving below the limits of tire traction are certainly contrary to our goal of getting around the track as fast as possible, so again, this is not really a factor.

Maximum track width is always set by rules in competition or by practical considerations on street vehicles, and unless you are running at very high speeds where aerodynamic drag is a big factor, you want to run the widest track width possible, so again this not a controllable factor. But the center of gravity, the point within the car where it, if suspended at that point, would be in perfect balance, can be altered. Maybe not much on some cars, but enough to affect performance. Simply keeping weight as low as possible in the car will lower the center of gravity, thus reducing weight transfer. This is very important to consider when modifying the suspension and lowering a car—which also lowers the center of gravity.

There are many misconceptions about weight transfer. Only the four items listed affect the amount of weight transfer. Body roll has a very minimal effect and should *not* be considered a factor. Dive and squat are not factors. Neither is the phase of the moon. So do not be misled into believing that anything other than the four factors listed to the left have an effect on the amount of weight transferred while cornering, braking, or accelerating.

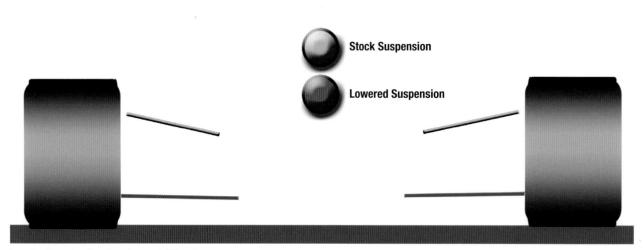

**Center of Gravity**
**Height above ground**

Stock Suspension

Lowered Suspension

Lowering the center of gravity reduces weight transfer.

Suspension geometry, even on a high tech, purpose-built race car, has no effect on weight transfer.

## ROLL COUPLE DISTRIBUTION

Roll couple is the total amount of roll resistance present in a car. Roll resistance is generated by the springs and anti-roll bars. Stiffer springs and anti-roll bars reduce body roll. Body roll is not necessarily a bad thing in itself, although it does cause some dynamics within the car that can hurt handling and overall performance. The most significant problems are increased camber change and aerodynamics.

Camber change causes the tire contact patch to become loaded unequally across the tire surface, even to the point that part of the tire contact patch loses contact with the road. This requires more negative camber to counteract, which can cause the same problem under straight line braking—part of the contact patch is not in firm contact with the road. Reducing body roll will reduce this effect. On the aero side, roll at the front allows more air under part of the car, causing aerodynamic lift and increasing aero drag. This is a big factor in competition and gets worse as speeds increase.

Body roll occurs when a car corners. Body roll is not caused by weight transfer, and reducing body roll does not reduce weight transfer. Weight transfer in corners occurs even with zero body roll, even with no suspension on the vehicle, such as a go-kart.

Where roll couple is the total amount of resistance to body roll provided by the springs and anti-roll bars at both front and rear, roll couple distribution is the amount of roll resistance at the front relative to the amount at the rear. Changing the roll couple distribution balance of the car changes the handling balance of the car. If we increase the front roll resistance, the handling balance will change. If the car was neutral before the change, the car will now understeer. If the car understeered prior to the change, it will understeer more; and if it oversteered, it will oversteer less after the change. The opposite effect occurs at the rear, where increasing rear roll resistance will increase oversteer or reduce understeer. The roll resistance can be increased by

This car is perfectly balanced, with neutral handling and the correct roll couple distribution.

This car shows mild understeer, meaning that front roll couple is too high.

increasing either the spring rates or the anti-roll bar rates, or both. This makes roll resistance changes the key to finding a perfect steady-state handling balance. Adjustable anti-roll bars allow fine-tuning of the roll couple distribution, making setup much easier.

While body roll is not directly related to the amount of weight transfer during cornering, roll couple distribution determines where the weight is transferred, front vs. rear, during cornering. Increasing front roll resistance forces more of the total weight being transferred to go to the front tires and less to the rear tires. Increasing rear roll resistance forces more of the weight being transferred to go to the rear tires. The load change on the tires, more at one end and less at the other, is what changes the handling balance. This works exactly the way you would expect based on the effects of vertical load on tire traction we discussed earlier.

Cars set up for drifting require extreme rear roll couple distribution in order to create extreme oversteer, the point of drifting. This amount of rear roll couple would make for a slow track car and rear tire wear would also be excessive. *Toyo Tire USA*

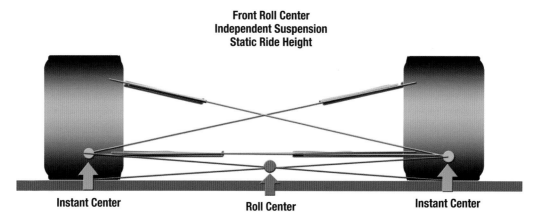

This illustration shows the roll center of the front suspension at rest.

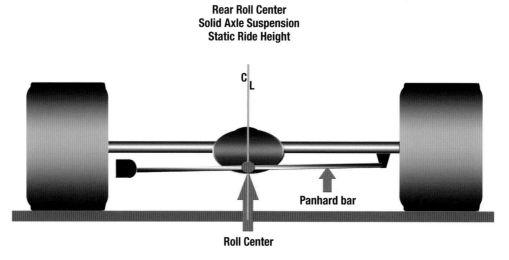

This illustration shows the roll center of the rear suspension at rest.

## BODY ROLL, ROLL CENTERS, ROLL AXIS, AND ROLL MIGRATION

During cornering, the lateral force created by tire traction causes body roll. This lateral force acts at the center of gravity. We have already seen that a lower center of gravity lowers the amount of weight transfer, the primary reason for lowering a car. Lowering also reduces the degree of body roll for a given cornering force.

When the body rolls during cornering, the suspension arms travel vertically because the suspension pivot points on the chassis are dropping (outside in a turn) or raising (inside in a turn). If you plot the suspension arms at rest, and extend lines through the lower and upper control arms, they will meet at a point (unless the arms are perfectly parallel) at a point called the "instant center." This point is nearly always toward the inside of the car. When you find the instant center for both left and right sides either front or rear, you can now plot the roll center, or the point that the suspension pivots around while cornering. The roll center is found by drawing a line from the instant center to the center of the tire contact patch at the ground. This is done on both left and right sides. Where the left side line intersects the right side line is called the roll center, the point that the suspension system rotates around during body roll.

**Front Roll Center Movement**
**Static no body roll**

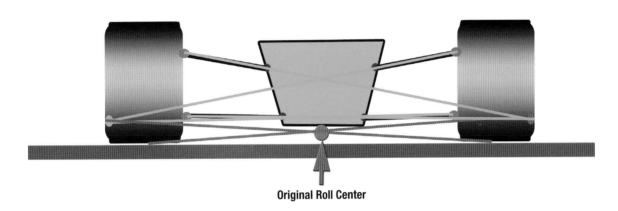

**Original Roll Center**

This illustration shows the roll center of the front suspension at rest with no body roll.

**Front Roll Center Movement**
**with 5 degrees of body roll**

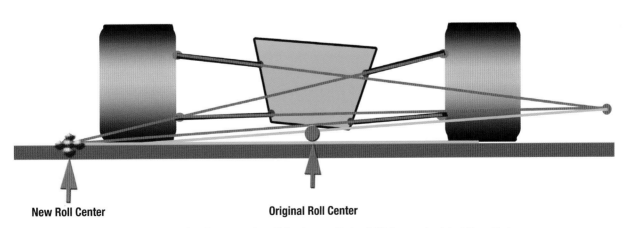

**New Roll Center**          **Original Roll Center**

This illustration shows extreme roll center movement of the front suspension with five degrees of body roll. This is unusual and should be avoided.

The roll center is not a fixed point. It can move vertically and horizontally during body roll, one of the reasons designing a suspension system is very difficult.

We have one more imaginary line. If you draw a line passing through the front roll center to the rear roll center, you have the roll axis, the axis that the chassis rotates around during cornering.

The amount of body roll in a corner is dependent on the cornering force and the distance between the roll axis and the center of gravity. A line from the roll axis to the center of gravity is called a moment arm and the longer the moment arm, the greater the force, and the higher the force, the greater the degree of body roll. The cornering force created by the tires acts at the center of gravity. This force creates a torque, just like a torque wrench, which will twist around the roll axis. If the roll axis passes through the center of gravity, there will be no body roll. If the roll axis is *above* the center of gravity, the body roll will be backward, which is never the case, but is possible.

Even though a high roll axis reduces body roll, high roll axis are not advantageous. Keep in mind that the job of the suspension control arms is to keep the tire contact patches on the ground so that the tires create maximum traction. This requires low roll centers and low roll axis, usually very close to the ground with the rear roll center slightly higher than the front roll center. This means more body roll and is why we need anti-roll bars.

The geometry of the upper and lower suspension control arms determines the roll centers, but it also determines the way in which the roll centers will move when the body rolls

in a corner. Suspension geometry engineers try to keep roll center movement to a minimum, usually within a box about 3 inches on each side. The center of the box is the roll center in a static state with the vehicle at rest.

If the roll center moves outside this 3-inch box, all kinds of problems occur, and the problems are worse the more the roll center moves. Vertical movement, called jacking, uses tire traction to try to lift or lower the chassis on the springs. This "jacking" reduces traction slightly, because more jacking means more of the tire traction is used to jack the car as opposed to going around a corner.

Lateral movement does not have much effect on traction directly, but can have a significant effect on driver feel. It is possible for the roll center to move laterally several *feet* as the body rolls in a corner. This is more likely with a strut type of suspension. When the roll axis swings laterally, it changes the relationship between the roll axis and the center of gravity. This can cause more or less body roll as the body is actually in the process of rolling. It also can change tire contact patch loading. These effects can change the roll couple distribution, or handling balance. The suspension geometry is also affected because body roll is changing on the fly and the suspension will continually be at a different point in the range of travel.

Since the loading and suspension geometry changes are both moving targets until the car takes a "set," or reaches the traction limits of the tires, the driver never gets a good feel for the traction limits of the car, making it difficult to drive fast. And the changing handling balance not only hurts driver feel, but also reduces total traction and makes the car slower around corners.

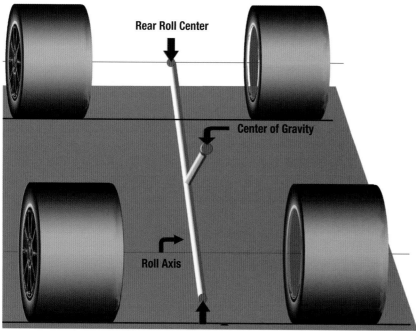

**Rear Roll Center**

**Center of Gravity**

**Roll Axis**

**Front Roll Center**

This illustration shows the front and rear roll centers, the line connecting them (called the roll axis), and the center of gravity. The line from the center of gravity to the roll axis is a moment arm acting like a torque wrench on the roll axis. The longer moment arm increases the torque caused by weight transfer, and this increases the amount of body roll. If the roll axis passes through the center of gravity, there will be no body roll, but that high of a roll axis causes more significant problems. The roll axis should be near the ground, slightly higher at the rear. Then anti-roll bars are used to control body roll.

This Scion was built by TRD for the Long Beach Toyota Pro/celebrity race. Progress built the suspension. *Progress Technology*

This Bonneville Honda from Progress Technology was the first sport compact to break the 200-mile-per-hour barrier at the fabled salt flats. Tire grip is at a premium on the rough salt surface, and a compliant suspension is crucial to insure maximum traction on the bumpy and slippery surface. *Progress Technology*

Here's an example: In the early 1990s, I was asked to prep and drive a Shelby CSX in the IMSA International Sedan Series. The CSX was a mid-sized front-wheel-drive platform with a turbocharged 2.2-liter four-cylinder engine putting out 225 horsepower. The cars in this series ran on DOT-legal race compound tires and several tire companies participated in the series. The series provided great racing. The Shelby factory had built and run the car for two years, barely running in the top 10. A privateer purchased the car. This was the first front-driver either of us had dealt with. We took the car to Willow Springs Raceway in California to test on the skid pad and street circuit. The car was terrible, lacking grip and very difficult to drive at the limit. It was not even averaging 1.0 g on the skid pad. The owner asked me to evaluate the suspension.

Suspension geometry computer software was new technology at the time. I used a program created by Wm. C. Mitchell called Racing by the Numbers™. It was state of the art for the day (and still is today with the latest version). When I plotted the front suspension geometry, I was both surprised and baffled by what I saw. The front roll center was moving over four feet to the outside of the car with only two degrees of body roll. It took a while to figure out what this was doing to the handling, but it was exactly as described earlier in the section. The rules stipulated that the suspension pivot points must remain stock. But this was an older car, by the series standards, being campaigned by a private entrant with a very limited budget. So I started moving pivot points on the lower control arm. It was a strut suspension system with no upper control arm, so everything had to be done on the lower arm. After trying many iterations on the computer, I found a geometry that limited lateral roll center movement to less than four inches, not great by today's standard, but a huge improvement.

Stiff springs have their advantages, but they can be a bit rough on the kidneys in certain situations. *Eibach Springs*

Honda Challenge front-drivers in action. *Toyo Tire USA*

This was done by moving the inner lower pivot inboard by less than a half inch and down about one-eighth inch. It wasn't legal, but it was better than scraping the car. The owner needed some top five finishes to collect enough prize money to keep racing.

While the car was being modified, we obtained a tire sponsor, General Tire. The fastest tire in the series was the BFGoodrich T/A treaded race compound street legal tire. The General tires had not been competitive. But we needed to make them work as well as the BFGs.

In the course of modifying the CSX, we spec'ed new springs, shocks, and anti-roll bars, with the rear bar being adjustable. I had done all of calculations for suspension frequencies and roll couple distribution. The adjustable rear bar was designed to lift the inside rear tire off the track surface slightly at the limit of traction. I did this because so much of the work being done by the tires was being done by the fronts, we only needed one rear tire while cornering. This proved to work very well.

When we went to test again, we started with the old BFGs. After dialing in camber and tire pressures, we cornered at 1.06 g,

a huge improvement. But the moment of truth would occur with the General Tires. We swapped tires, readjusted tire pressures (different designs of tires require different tire pressures and camber settings) and we reached the same g-force as with the older and worn BFGs. At least we were in the ballpark. The CSX understeered a little more than the BFGs, so we stiffened the rear anti-roll bar a notch. The car was nearly perfectly neutral, and the inside rear tire was about a half inch off the track surface. The cornering force improved to 1.07 g, likely better than any other car in the series.

The CSX became competitive, running in the top five even with an engine about 15 horsepower less than the factory teams using the same engine from Dodge and Mitsubishi. The car never won, but did accomplish several top five finishes.

Today, car manufacturers do a much better job of engineering suspension geometry, so the radical lateral movement of the roll centers is not very likely. But this really shows how difficult it is to engineer suspension systems, and why good engineering and track testing are so important.

## WHY SO MANY MODERN RACE CARS HAVE EXTREMELY STIFF SPRINGS

When Honda front drivers started appearing on racetracks in the late 1980s, little was known about making front drive passenger cars work in this environment. The early Civics and CRXs were good cars, but they suffered from the same problems, and more, that I experienced with the Shelby CSX. But when these cars were first on the racetrack, little was known, at least among racers, about suspension frequencies and roll center migration. Yet it was obvious from tire wear patterns that something bad was occurring with the suspension geometry. The front tires were only wearing on the edge of the tread, an indication of camber change, as well as some other issues. Since rules did not allow modifications to the suspension geometry, the racers tried to limit body roll and its associated problems by running stiffer springs. And the stiffer the springs, the better the cars worked. Eventually, the springs neared three times stiffer than the stock springs. This worked because it virtually eliminated any body roll, which negated any issues with camber change or roll center movement. But the ride quality was terrible, and it took exceptional driving talent to control these little beasts. And in that era, some very talented drivers emerged, including Dorsey Schroeder, Parker Johnstone, and Bob Endicott. These guys figured out how to drive these rock hard platforms very quickly, and their success on the track set the precedent for very stiff springs on front drive compact cars modified for road racing.

In this era, all of these cars used strut suspension systems, which are very inexpensive to manufacture. But as described in the Shelby CSX story earlier, the strut cars have inherent problems with geometry. Today, however, many front drivers use control arms, and most of the issues have been eliminated. Today, using sensible suspension frequencies, so that the tire contact patches stay on the road surface over bumps, is the best approach. Ultra stiff springs are just not necessary, and actually are a detriment to ultimate performance. So let's take a closer look at spring rates, wheel rates and suspension frequencies.

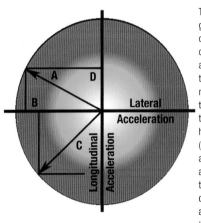

The traction circle is a graphic representation of tire traction used for cornering, braking, and acceleration. The line around the circumference is the maximum amount of traction the tires can make. Cornering traction is along the horizontal axis with braking (from the center down) and acceleration along the vertical axis. In the illustration, "A" is the vector force showing a combination of cornering "B" and acceleration "D." The line "C" is the vector force where braking and cornering are both taking place.

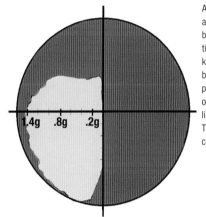

A driver's goal when attempting fast laps should be to use all of the possible tire traction. This means keeping the force plot shown by the blue area as close as possible to the circumference of the circle. Acceleration is limited by power, not traction. This driver is doing okay, but could be going faster.

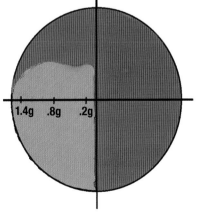

Here the driver is right on the edge of the circumference and right on the limits of tire traction.

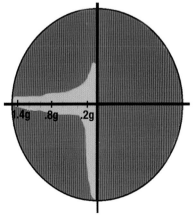

Here the driver is not using the tires' capabilities at all. He is never braking and turning, or accelerating or turning at the same time. Considerable speed is being left on the table here.

The traction circle illustrates just how important the driver is in the overall equation. What the driver needs to do with the controls will be covered in another chapter. *Shutterstock*

## WHEEL RATES AND SUSPENSION FREQUENCIES

The wheel rate of a spring is the rate acting at the tire contact patch. The wheel rate is determined by both the leverage of the suspension control arms acting on the spring and the actual distance traveled by the spring versus the distance traveled by the tire contact patch when the suspension moves vertically. This is called the motion ratio.

The frequency of a suspension system is the rate at which it vibrates or oscillates over a bump and is expressed in cycles per second. The frequency is determined by the wheel rate of a spring and the sprung weight resting on that spring. The frequency number can be used to compare any car's spring rates to any other car's spring rates. While knowing a spring rate of someone else's car is useless information, knowing the frequency is extremely helpful, given the data comes from a car with excellent handling characteristics.

The topics of wheel rates and frequencies is covered in greater detail in chapter 8.

## TRACTION CIRCLE

The traction circle is a graphic representation of tire traction used for cornering, braking, and acceleration. Tires can make traction in any direction: forward for acceleration, rearward for braking, and laterally for cornering. The rubber molecules at the tire contact patch do not know or care which direction they work in. For this reason, all of a tire's traction can be used in one direction, or part can be used for cornering and part for either braking or acceleration. See chapter 9 for more about this.

## THE DRIVER

Often overlooked as a vehicle dynamics factor, the driver is actually a major factor. The driver controls when dynamic events occur based on when the driver uses one or more of the controls. And the driver determines, at least in part, how quickly dynamic events occur based on how fast and abruptly the driver uses the controls. Many drivers are too abrupt with control inputs and upset the dynamic balance of the chassis, which degrades overall vehicle performance.

## THE OVERALL GOAL

If you're competing, it is important to keep in mind that the singular goal is to get around (or down) the racetrack as fast as possible, whether for a single lap or an entire race. For the street and highway, improving handling balance and braking performance makes your vehicle more fun to drive and improves safety. Vehicle dynamics relates ultimately to tire traction at the tire contact patch. Optimizing traction on the complete car means faster lap times, less tire wear, and safer highway driving. We can do this by manipulating the chassis components and the driver's steering, braking, and accelerator inputs. For cars used primarily on the street, additional factors must be considered when modifying suspension. Ride comfort, suspension travel, ground clearance, and noise levels are factors we will consider later.

## WHAT'S POSSIBLE

Street car-based race cars are limited by rules like tire size and type, suspension modifications, and weight. But many stock-based race cars can achieve cornering forces in excess of 1.0 g, many in excess of 1.4 g. But what about on the street? What is really possible? In the project car section of this book, we have two street cars, both front drive Honda daily drivers, both capable of 1 g of cornering force. To do that they were on DOT-legal race compound tires. These tires wear quickly due to the soft rubber compounds, but they could be used on the street. With ultra high performance tires, the magic 1.0 g mark was not achieved, but both cars got close enough that they would scare the average passenger silly on an interstate ramp. For all practical purposes, 0.95 g would have the same effect. That level of grip is awesome for any street-driven vehicle.

Let's gain a little perspective. A Formula One car corners in high speed turns at 3.5 g, an Indy Car at 2.5 g, and a British Touring Car at about 1.5 g. The F1 and Indy cars have enough downforce at 190 miles per hour to triple the load on their tires. That accounts for most of the traction. A British Touring Car races on slicks. They all have state of the art, extremely rigid chassis structures, sophisticated suspension systems, and none of them would last 30 seconds on the streets we drive each day. So, any car that can be comfortably driven on the streets and highways of your neighborhood and exceed 1.0 g cornering force is quite a machine.

Just what is 1.0 g of cornering force? 1.0 g is the force of gravity and equals an acceleration of 32.2 feet per second squared. Remember the science class question, "What falls faster, a pound of lead or a pound of feathers?" The answer is that they both fall at the same rate. That rate is 1.0 g. But g forces apply to more than falling objects. Acceleration, deceleration, and changes in direction all create forces and we can compare the forces to the force of gravity. When it comes to going around corners at 1.0 g, it means that the tires are making traction equivalent to the weight of the car. If a 2,500-pound car corners at 1.0 g, the tires are making 2,500 pounds of traction. That's why 1.0 g of cornering force is so significant and considered the ultimate benchmark for cornering and handling performance.

1.0 g is the equivalent of the four-minute mile in track, going 200 miles per hour at Bonneville, or running a sub-ten-second quarter mile. It's like pulling 8 g in an F-16 fighter. A 1.0 g cornering force on a skid pad is a significant accomplishment. To reach 1.0 g on a street machine with DOT street legal tires is even more significant. And to do so within the confines of the stock, unmodified wheel wells adds to the challenge.

To put this into time perspective, 30 years ago, the Trans-Am Camaro campaigned by Roger Penske and driven by the legendary Mark Donahue could barely muster a two-way average of 0.90 g on the skid pad. Even most of today's supercars are unable to reach that magic 1.0-g threshold. But some of today's fairly average cars like the Subaru WRX, Mitsubishi Evo, and Mustang, with simple suspension modifications and ultra high performance tires are able to pull 1.0-g lateral acceleration on the skid pad.

Purpose-built race cars with rock hard suspension and super-sticky, super-wide racing slicks like NASCAR Sprint Cup cars pull about 1.3 g on the skid pad. For a street car to run at 1.0-g lateral acceleration is a considerable achievement. And that can be done with a reasonable ride and a minimal compromise. And a 1.0-g street ride makes a great occasional track day car.

Formula One cars (top), Indy Cars (center), and British Touring Cars (above) can all exceed the 1.0 g limit. *Shutterstock*

# Chapter 4
# Tires

The single biggest improvement in handling performance comes from tires. The improvement is even greater when combined with a coordinated suspension package and the proper wheels for the application. But high performance tires, and ultra high performance tires wear faster, so the cost per mile driven increases. And tires are expendable items, more so than any other component in the suspension system. So tires are a relatively expensive proposition.

When it comes to tires, traction is increased when the tire rubber compound is softer and when the tire contact patch is bigger. The tread design and sidewall construction also play a role in allowing the tire contact patch to work on the road surface and maintain contact with the surface. Even the softest tire will not achieve good results if the tread design and sidewall construction miss the mark. Many factors come into play when selecting tires for improved handling.

## PERFORMANCE VS. COST

Tires are not cheap, but dollar for dollar, they offer the single biggest handling performance improvement. Performance tires cost less than high performance tires and ultra high performance tires cost the most. Race compound tires actually cost slightly less outright, but even more important than outright expense is the cost per mile. Performance tires have softer rubber compounds than OE tires, meaning that they will wear out more quickly even driven the same way. Ultra high performance tires wear the quickest of the tires designed for highway driving. They also cost the most of the possible choices. Ultra high performance tires will last for upwards of 20,000 miles when driven hard or used for an occasional autocross or track day event. Better mileage is possible if you drive easier.

Everything we do is for the purpose of keeping the vertical load equal on all four tire contact patches and equal across each tire contact patch as much of the time as possible. Of course that is not always possible as with this Nissan endurance racer at the Nürburgring. *Falken Tire*

Like many tire companies, Toyo offers a complete line of high performance, ultra high performance, max performance, and DOT street legal race compound tires. *Toyo Tire USA*

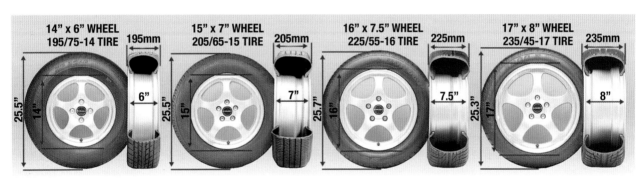

The plus-sizing concept allows tires to be mounted on a different rim diameter without changing the diameter of the tire. *Tire Rack*

## ULTRA HIGH PERFORMANCE TIRES VS. PERFORMANCE TIRES

There are great compromises available in most manufacturers' product lines in the high performance arena that give good performance and excellent wear. But to really improve handling performance the ultra high performance tires are in another world, one worth the expense if you really enjoy high performance driving. As a bonus, the performance level also improves safety.

## PLUS SIZING

Plus sizing is a convenient way to categorize tires larger in wheel diameter and width for similar applications. When going up in tire size, or plus sizing, the wheel diameter increases, as does the width. The width increase means a bigger tire contact patch on the road surface for improved traction. The wheel diameter increase is accommodated by a shorter sidewall height, keeping the diameter of the tire,

or more importantly the rolling circumference of the tires, nearly equal to the original tire. This allows the suspension geometry, anti-lock brake sensors, gear ratio, and speedometer to function unaltered, unlike a change in tire diameter would cause. When plus sizing, it is both desirable and necessary to increase the section width as well. It is desirable because it also means an increase in contact patch area. It is necessary to maintain similar air volume within the tire when mounted on a wheel. Reducing the sidewall height while keeping the same diameter reduces the sidewall area. If the tread width remains stock, then the volume of air within the tire is reduced and the tire will not have the same characteristics. Increasing the tread width increases the area and compensates for the reduction of sidewall height. This allows the air volume to remain nearly the same as stock. The advantage of plus sizing in addition to improved looks is the increase in tire contact patch area and more traction. The disadvantage is increased ride harshness.

## TIRE AND WHEEL SIZING

It is important that the proper wheel width be used for a given tire size. Tire companies provide data for each tire they make, including wheel width recommendations. The range is usually about two inches in wheel width, with the middle width a good compromise for highway use. Using a rim outside the recommended range can be very dangerous. If the rim is too narrow, the tire contact patch will crown and the sidewall beads will not seat properly. This could cause the tire to unseat from the wheel rim, causing the tire to deflate. This will ruin the tire at minimum and cause a crash in the worst case scenario. Putting a tire on a rim that is too wide can cause the same problem, though the tire will never seat properly on the rim bead and may never inflate.

Within the range of recommended wheel widths for a specific tire, the wider wheel choice is best. When a tire is on the widest recommended wheel, the tire contact patch is the most equally loaded. For highway driving, the middle wheel width will work, but for competition, the widest wheel is best. For a specific competition class where wheel width is limited, using a tire with a smaller cross section width is often better than trying to use the widest tire that will fit in the fender well on a rim that is narrower than optimum.

For performance applications, using the narrowest recommended wheel width is not desirable because the tire contact patch is slightly crowned. This is not dangerous relative to the tire bead staying seated to the rim, but it does hurt overall traction. Additionally, a rim on the narrow side of the recommended range can cause the tire contact patch to chatter or skip during cornering as the limit of traction is approached. For this reason, select the widest rim recommended for a specific tire application.

But you can go too far on wheel rim width, a trend becoming popular in several forms of motorsport. The practice is dangerous, since a tire bead can become unseated from the rim bead, causing a loss of pressure and a sudden change in handling. This can often lead to a crash.

The reason why this trend has become popular is that it's seen as a way to overcome handling issues caused by excessively stiff spring rates, another popular practice. As explained elsewhere in this book, the job of the springs is to allow compliance of the tire contact patch with the racing surface. It is *not* the job of the tire sidewall to act as a primary spring because the suspension springs are too stiff. While tire sidewalls are designed to flex proportionally to tire pressure, they are not designed to work as a cantilever, which they must do on a wheel that is too wide. By angling the tire sidewall on a too wide wheel, the effective spring rate of the sidewall is decreased, causing it to flex more under the same load. This flexing improves tire contact patch compliance, which is why handling is improved. *But,* it also accelerates tire sidewall wear, makes the sidewall more susceptible to damage and punctures, and increases the likelihood of the tire bead unseating from the rim. It is much better to utilize the proper

Aftermarket wheels look great, but when choosing them also consider strength and weight, especially for use on the track or autocross course. *Progress Technology*

Most tire manufacturers offer a wide array of performance tires to fit any number of applications. The following selections are from Toyo Tire's extensive line of performance rubber. The Toyo Proxes 1 is built for many of the most powerful cars in the world. *Toyo Tire USA*

Ideal for road racing, track days, and high performance driving schools, the Proxes R888 is the next-generation, street legal competition tire from Toyo Tires. *Toyo Tire USA*

The Proxes RA1 is a street legal competition tire that features high-tech components to provide an uncommon advantage to the cost-conscious competitor who still demands quick lap times. *Toyo Tire USA*

The new Proxes TQ is a street legal drag radial that keeps the power to the ground on high horsepower muscle cars and street machines. *Toyo Tire USA*

The Proxes R1R provides extreme performance for serious street driving in sports coupes and sedans. *Toyo Tire USA*

The Proxes T1R is an ultra-high performance tire designed exclusively for high-end sport sedans and coupes. *Toyo Tire USA*

spring rates for the optimum suspension frequency for the track and vehicle characteristics. In the long run, the ultimate performance is enhanced and the cost is greatly reduced, considering that, sooner or later, a tire will unseat from the rim and a costly crash is likely.

## TIRE CLEARANCE

A lack of tire clearance is both costly and dangerous. A rubbing tire can wear through and blow out. At a minimum, tire wear is accelerated. Most tire shops specializing in ultra high performance tires know how to properly fit wheel/tire combinations for specific applications. Many tire and wheel manufacturers, along with some retailers and mail order dealers, have web sites with fitment guides that will tell you what will work for your specific vehicle.

## RIDE VS. PERFORMANCE

Ultra high performance tires are more responsive and provide improved grip. One of the ways this is accomplished is by utilizing stiffer sidewall construction. Additionally, plus sizing means shorter sidewalls which further increases tire sidewall stiffness. This translates into increased ride harshness. Going from an original tire to an ultra high performance tire increases ride harshness. Going to a plus-one tire size increases harshness more and plus-two sizing will further increase harshness.

The trade-off is more traction and especially better responsiveness vs. ride quality degradation. Add stiffer suspension components and less suspension bump travel and the ride can become downright stiff, even uncomfortable. A very aggressive package can mean some level of discomfort on bumpy roads, so carefully consider your priorities before taking the plunge.

## RACE COMPOUND DOT TIRES

Race compound DOT street legal tires make gobs of traction—in the dry! In the wet, forget it. You may as well have bald tires on ice. They also wear very quickly, often wearing completely in 10,000 miles of normal street and highway driving (although I've never met anyone driving on race compound DOT tires who drives normally). Between the wear and the poor wet traction, these tires are best left to track days, autocrossing, and racing. If you have a dual purpose vehicle, save the race compound tires for the track and get to the track on a high or ultra high performance tire.

## WET VS. DRY TRACTION

One of the design considerations for a tire manufacturer is dry traction vs. wet traction. Most original equipment tires have a compromise design that allows good dry traction combined with good wet traction. These tires have tread patterns that work well in the wet, but reduce steering responsiveness in dry situations. High and ultra high performance tires have softer tread compounds and much more aggressive tread patterns, which usually means a higher void ratio, the area of the tire contact patch that has rubber on the road vs. the area of the grooves at the tire contact patch. Higher void ratios mean more

The Proxes 4 is an all-season, M&S rated, ultra high performance tire designed primarily for plus-fitment applications on sport compact cars, sports sedans, and coupes. *Toyo Tire USA*

The Toyo Proxes drag slick *Toyo Tire USA*

Continental Tire is leading the way in developing ultra high performance tires for wet and snowy conditions. *Continental Tire*

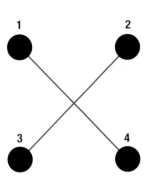
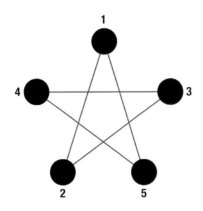
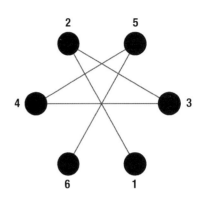

The wheel lug patterns show the proper tightening sequence for wheel lug nuts or bolts. *Tire Rack*

resistance to hydroplaning but less rubber on the ground. Lower void ratios increase traction but also offer less resistance to hydroplaning. Original equipment tires have higher void ratios with performance tires, high performance tires and ultra high performance tires have smaller and smaller void ratios.

Wet traction is influenced by the tread compound as well. Ultra high performance tires with higher amounts of silica compound provide better grip in the wet. This usually reduces dry traction slightly; but if you live in a rainy environment, the trade-off is a good one.

Wider tires are also less resistant to hydroplaning. More rubber on the road, whether from greater section width or lower void ratio, means more hydroplaning. Additionally, wider tires do not track as well over longitudinal grooves, expansion strips, and road repairs. While this is mostly an annoyance in the dry, it can be very edgy in wet weather. If you live in a rainy area, or have a severe rainy season, have a second set of tires for bad weather. And if you deal with snow and/or mud, snow tires are the only way to go for the best grip possible.

## TIRE CARE

While today's tires are very durable, there are several items to be aware of to get the most wear, reliability, and safety from your tires.

* Keep your tires at the proper inflation pressure at all times
* Avoid hitting curbs
* Check sidewalls for damage regularly

If you have a second set of tires for track days, autocrossing, wet weather, or winter driving, put the set off the car in green or black plastic trash bags for storage. This reduces the weathering effects and helps keep the tires more supple and keeps the tread compound from hardening as quickly over time.

## TIRE FEEL AND DRIVABILITY

Every tire has a personality of its own. And some drivers prefer certain characteristics in a tire. While the grip of a tire comes from the tread compound and design, the personality lives in the sidewall construction. Some tires are instantly responsive to steering inputs. They provide solid feedback through the controls and the seat of the driver's pants. They are predictable and it's easy to be smooth and consistent.

On the other hand, some tires feel like rubber bands, constantly expanding and contracting. Just about the time you think the tire is going to stabilize, it feels like the sidewall springs back and the handling balance is totally altered. It's hard to drive fast consistently on tires like that. And they certainly do not instill confidence.

A fairly stiff tire sidewall that is linear in its response to steering inputs and has a good tread pattern design makes a tire that is both predictable and stable in its feel. These tires can be a joy to drive.

This cutaway of a Bridgestone Potenza DOT race tire show some of what goes into the construction of a tire.

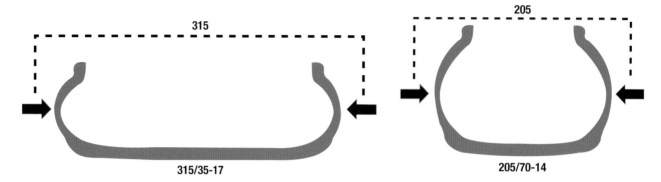

315

315/35-17

205

205/70-14

These illustrations show the difference between a low and high profile tire. *Tire Rack*

## SPRING RATES OF TIRE SIDEWALLS

Over the last 40 years, I have been involved in several tire comparison tests, some for DOT race tires. In every case the methodology was flawed. I was always adamant that the test vehicle be tuned to the tires, but this was too costly and time-consuming. But not doing so invalidated the tests. I have also encountered many racers who change tire brands, either by choice or because of a change to spec tire rules. In most cases, the racer complained about how bad the new tire is compared to the existing tire. In fact, the new tire could have been better. Here are the issues and why re-tuning the platform for the new tire is crucial.

The sidewall of a tire is flexible. If it wasn't, it would not steer around corners with very much speed. Every tire has a sidewall spring rate which is affected by the design, construction method, and the pressure used in the tire. Changing from one brand of tire to another, or when the manufacturer comes out with a new tire design, you can be pretty sure that the sidewall construction is different, and that means that the spring rate of the sidewall will be different at a given tire pressure. In fact, you can take two identical tires from the same manufacturer and they will likely have slightly different sidewall spring rates.

If you have been contemplating this as you read, you may already understand the issue here. If the tire sidewalls have a spring rate, it must work in conjunction with the springs and anti-roll bars, and therefore will have an effect on the roll couple distribution, or handling balance of the platform. And this is true and the core of the problem.

Since most of the roll couple on a car is distributed to the front, usually in the 60 to 85 percent range on a production-based race car, then a change in tire sidewall spring rates that is the same front to rear will alter the roll couple percentage front to rear. This will change the handling balance. And this will require a change to the anti-roll bar rates and possibly the spring rates as well.

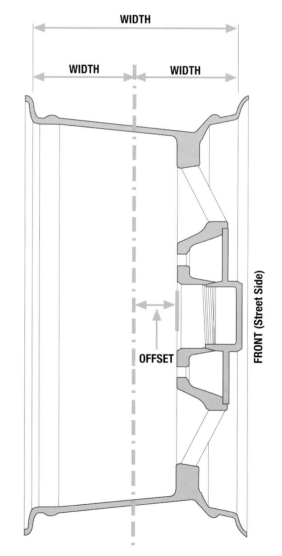

WIDTH

WIDTH WIDTH

OFFSET

FRONT (Street Side)

This diagram explains wheel offset terminology. *Tire Rack*

# HOW TIRES MAKE TRACTION

Most racers understand that tires make traction through friction between the rubber molecules at the tire contact patch and the racing surface. And most of us understand that traction increases as vertical load on the tire increases, which is why aerodynamic downforce works so well. In addition, most racers understand that the tire will make more traction if the entire contact patch is equally loaded, which is why monitoring tire temperatures is useful. Within this basic knowledge are misconceptions and misinformation that can add confusion to an already difficult topic. Let's see if some light can be shed on the topic.

In this discussion we will not address tire design or construction, since no one I know who races can change those parameters anyway. Let's start with the factors within the tire that affect traction. These are the only factors within the tire affecting traction:

* Basic tire design and construction
* Sidewall rigidity
* Tread rubber compound
* Tread design (especially on dirt)
* Tire size

Most of us run on a spec tire, so none of these factors are under our control. Even if tires are open, size, compound, and possibly tread design are the only choices we have, and those are limited.

There are also factors we have control over. These include:

* Tire pressure
* Tire camber
* Tire toe-in (or out)
* Camber change

Each of these items has an optimum setting which allows the tire to create maximum traction for a given set of circumstances.

Then there is the vertical load on the tire, which is crucial to understand, but also the most misunderstood element of tire traction. Traction increases as the vertical load on the tire increases. But it is very important to understand that the relation to vertical load and traction is not linear. Being non-linear means that if the load on the tire is increased, while the traction also increases, it does not increase as much as the load. For example, if the vertical load is doubled, then the traction increase is somewhat less than doubled. If the vertical load increased, say 200 pounds, the traction increase may only be about 175 pounds. This is a good time to more clearly explain traction in terms of pounds of force and vertical load on a tire. We'll start with traction.

One way to look at traction is in pounds of force. The most convenient way to do this is to look at the entire car as a whole, and measure the force that the tires create. Most racers have heard the term g-force. If a car accelerates at 1.0 g, and the car weighs 3,000 pounds, then the tires are producing 3,000 pounds of traction force. This applies to acceleration forward, braking (negative acceleration) and cornering (lateral acceleration). A late-model stock car can produce a cornering force of about 1.4 g in a flat corner, about 1.25 g under braking and somewhere around 0.50 g acceleration on a short track with a very low final drive ratio. For a 3,000-pound car cornering at 1.4 g, the traction in pounds is 4,200 pounds (3,000 x 1.4 = 4,200). That is a lot of force from those four tire contact patches.

Vertical load is the load actually seen at the tire contact patch. This includes the weight resting on the tire contact patch *plus* any aerodynamic downforce. If the car creates any aerodynamic lift, then the vertical load on the tire will be less than the weight on the tire, since the car is lifting instead of being pushed down. Aerodynamic downforce is good because it increases traction *without* increasing the weight of the car. Let's look more closely at this, since this is another area of some confusion.

Downforce is pretty much a traction freebee. It costs a little in acceleration at high speeds, and reduces top speed somewhat, but it adds no *weight* to the car. Adding weight to the car actually reduces the relative amount of traction compared to the total weight of the vehicle. In the previous example, the 3,000-pound car made 4,200 pounds of cornering force at the limit. Let's say we add 500 pounds

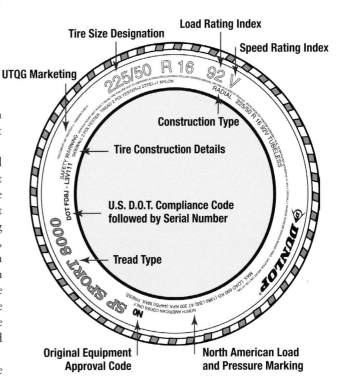

Here the markings on the tire sidewall are defined. *Tire Rack*

Tire testing is the critical element in tuning tires and the suspension; it is really the only means of getting the best from your tires and suspension. Here the team from Progress Technology is testing an Acura RSX at Auto Club Speedway in Fontana, California. *Progress Technology*

to the car with nothing else changed, including the weight distribution. It's easy to understand that the car will not accelerate as quickly because it weighs more and the engine is making the same horsepower. It is less obvious that cornering speed will reduce. Here's why: The 500 pounds of weight adds 500 pounds of vertical load to the tires, but, because the relationship between the vertical load increase and traction increase is not linear, the amount of traction increase will only be about 400 pounds. That means the tires now make an additional 560 pounds of traction (400 x 1.4) for a total of 4,760 pounds of traction. This works out to a cornering force of only 1.36 g. This equates to a loss in cornering speed due only to the effect on the tires, not on the dynamics of the suspension. This is due entirely to the characteristic of tires where traction does not increase as fast as load.

This non-linear relationship also becomes more significant as the design load of the tire is approached. In other words, if a tire has a maximum load capacity of 2,000 pounds, but normally carries only 750 pounds, doubling the load to 1,500 is approaching the design limit. Here the traction may only increase by about half the extra load. If the design load is exceeded, the situation gets worse. While there is nothing you can actually do to a tire or suspension to change this non-linear relationship, there are plenty of factors you need to understand in order to minimize its effect and allow your race car to create the maximum possible amount of traction.

These factors are crucial to maximize traction for each individual tire:

- Camber angle at the front
- Stagger at the rear (one tire is taller than the other tire)
- Tire pressure at each tire
- Toe settings front and rear (axle housing squareness)
- Roll steer and axle squareness at the rear
- Bump steer at the front

Many factors contribute to traction, such as construction characteristics, design, peak slip angles, and track conditions. The things controlled to some degree by the enthusiast, like weight distribution and chassis setup, make all of the difference in handling. In motorsports, the team making best use of the potential traction at all four tires is the team with the best chance to win.

The uniform goal in every case is to have the entire tire contact patch equally loaded across the surface of the contact patch. If the entire contact patch is not equally loaded, you are not getting all the traction possible from that tire. If you look at the tire contact patch as a series of one-inch squares, one square compared to another acts just like one tire compared to another. Reducing the load on one square increases the load on another square. The square losing load loses traction more quickly than the other square gains traction from the increased load. In other words, the tire contact patch as a whole is making less traction than it could be if the contact patch was equally loaded over its entire area. This is hard to achieve, but the team doing the best job has its tires working the best.

Once you have the entire tire contact patch at each corner working to its maximum traction potential, then the goal is to get all four tires creating the maximum amount of traction possible for the whole vehicle. To accomplish this requires an understanding of weight transfer.

Weight transfer occurs anytime that the tires create a force. Acceleration, braking, and cornering are the three axes on which weight transfer occurs. Only four factors affect the amount of weight transfer. Using cornering as an example, those factors are:

- Center of gravity height above ground
- Track width
- Cornering speed vs. turn radius
- Vehicle weight

A higher center of gravity means more weight transfer. So does a narrower track width, higher cornering speeds and higher vehicle weight. So why is weight transfer a problem? More weight transfer means a greater load change on the tire contact patches. Some tires lose load, some gain load. And just like we have seen previously, that non-linear relationship means that maximum potential traction occurs only when all four tires are equally loaded. A tire losing weight will lose traction more quickly than the tire gaining weight will gain traction. That equals a net reduction from the maximum possible traction. So we want to minimize weight transfer as much as possible for starters.

To reduce weight transfer means keeping the center of gravity as low as possible. We also want to keep the track width as wide as allowed, although other factors must be considered, like handling balance, aerodynamics, and racing surface conditions. We want to run at minimum weight or as light as possible if there is no minimum. The only thing contrary to performance is going through turns slower than possible, so eliminate that as a way to reduce weight transfer.

In addition to reducing the amount of weight transfer, we must also look at static weight distribution and how that affects weight transfer. If you road race, then 50/50 left/right weight distribution is desirable. Why? Let's say you run 55 percent left weight on a road course. The car will be faster in left turns than in the equivalent right turns. Taking into account weight transfer in the turns, in a left turn, the inside will lose weight and the outside (right) gains the weight so that in the turn the dynamic weight distribution is about 50/50. That is near the ideal situation. But in a right turn, the dynamic weight distribution becomes 60 percent left, 40 percent right. This means the right side tires are not working very hard and the cornering force is much lower.

On an oval, where we only turn left, the same criteria apply, but we aren't so concerned about right turn cornering force. So what is ideal? A perfect 50/50 side to side and front to rear dynamic weight distribution in steady state cornering situations allows the maximum amount of cornering traction. Anything less than this means an uneven load on the tires and less than maximum possible traction. The goal then is to have the correct amount of static left side weight so that the weight that transfers to the right in a left turn creates a dynamic weight distribution of 50/50. How do you know this? Tire temperatures. First they should be within 10 degrees F across the tread surface so that each tire is optimized. Then the average temperature of each tire should be within five degrees of the other three tires. This is difficult to achieve, especially at the left front, but that is the goal.

Weight transfer is much less of a problem fore and aft during braking and acceleration since the wheelbase is longer than the track width and resists weight transfer better. A disparity up to 5 percent in front to rear static weight distribution is not much of a concern. If front or rear static weight exceeds 55 percent, then the tire size (actually the area of the contact patch) at the heavy end should increase to compensate for the higher vertical load.

Many factors contribute to traction, like construction characteristics, design, peak slip angles and track conditions. The factors controlled to some degree by the racer, like weight distribution and chassis setup, make all of the difference on the racetrack. The team making best use of the potential traction at all four tires is the team with the best chance to win.

# Chapter 5
# Suspension Modifications

To achieve improved handling performance, a complete system including wheels, tires, springs, anti-roll bars, shocks, and bushings must be designed for a specific application. It's not a matter of grabbing parts and bolting them on the car; an effective system must utilize components that are designed to work together. And it doesn't matter if the car is designed for road racing, rallying, autocrossing, track days, or just street driving; the package should be designed for the type of vehicle and the activities that the vehicle will be used for. Here are some priorities.

## FOR COMPETITION
- Maximum traction
- Adequate suspension travel and optimum suspension frequencies for surface conditions
- Responsiveness to driver control inputs
- Class rules
- Driver comfort

*Progress Technology*

*Eibach Springs*

A complete system including wheels, tires, springs, anti-roll bars, shocks, and bushings must be designed for a specific application, such as for this competition BMW. *Progress Technology*

Some cars, like this street BMW, have excellent suspension from the factory, requiring aftermarket suspension components only for specific use on the track. *Eibach Springs*

Cars used for street and track require some modification to at least allow adjustments to ride height and to improve handling balance. *Eibach Springs*

## FOR PERFORMANCE STREET APPLICATIONS ONLY

- Adequate suspension travel
- Ground clearance
- Occupant comfort
- Overall traction
- Responsiveness to driver control inputs

## FOR DUAL PURPOSE VEHICLES (STREET PLUS AUTOCROSS/TRACK DAYS)

All of the above are priorities, but not in the same order. The best case is to have one set of street wheels/tires and another set for track use. Coilover suspension allows ride height adjustments easily. An adjustable anti-roll bar allows fine tuning of handling balance for the track. Urethane suspension bushings allow a good compromise between ride harshness and quick responsiveness.

In all of the above cases, the system and all of its components must be matched or designed to work together to achieve the desired results. Several companies provide excellent packages to achieve any desired of level of performance. And an experienced tuning shop will provide the expertise needed to create the best possible package for your needs.

## STREET PACKAGES

If your goal is to improve street handling performance, a package designed for that purpose is needed to achieve all of the desired compromises. On the handling side of the performance equation, we are attempting to improve cornering and braking performance without destroying ride quality. The aggressive nature of the wheel/tire combo should provide the necessary traction and responsiveness that a performance enthusiast is looking for, but without the suspension modifications, the tire contact patches will not comply with the road surface correctly. The increased traction causes body roll to increase, and that causes even more camber change during cornering. More camber means less of the tire contact patch is firmly contacting the road surface, so traction is less than it could be. By controlling the body roll with stiffer springs and anti-roll bars, camber change decreases and the tire contact patches comply with the road surface more firmly. But there are trade-offs.

A fully adjustable coil-over package is best for track use. *Eibach Springs*

A simple spring and antiroll bar kit can improve highway handling and is good for occasional track day use. The adjustable anti-roll bars allow fine tuning for the track. *Eibach Springs*

A well-engineered kit with no adjustments is ideal for improved highway handling performance. *Eibach Springs*

With stiffer springs and shocks along with low profile plus-sized tires and wheels, the ride quality is compromised. Lowering a car improves appearance and cornering, but ride deteriorates due to less suspension travel and stiffer components. And the reduction in ground clearance also causes problems with scraping over bumps, ruts, and driveways. The key is finding a company that makes the best package for your application.

Several project cars I have been involved with have achieved 1.0 g cornering or have come very close. To get a car to corner at or near 1.0 g is all about traction and controlling that traction. The traction comes from the tires. The rubber compound and the area of the tire contact patches are the key factors. Add more rubber to the road, and the traction increases. Make the rubber softer and the traction increases, but so does tire wear. But bigger, softer tires are only part of the story. If the tire contact patches do not stay in touch with the road surface, traction is reduced, or even lost. The suspension system must be designed to allow those sticky tires to work in a variety of road and driving conditions.

For example, the springs have two jobs. First, they need to keep the car from bottoming either on the road surface or on the suspension linkages. If you lower a car, then the springs must be stiffer to control this. But that hurts ride quality if you go too far. Second, the springs must allow the tire contact patch to stay on the road surface over bumps. If a spring is too stiff for a given bump, the tire loses compliance with the road. This ruins traction and handling performance. But if a spring is too soft, body roll is excessive and the tire contact patch will lean, meaning that some of the patch is not loaded and that too reduces traction. Anti-roll bars must be designed to work with a given spring combination to control roll and help keep that tire contact flat on the road surface during cornering.

Custom sub-frames, like this one from Hotchkis for a 1968–1969 Camaro, can eliminate suspension geometry issues while improving strength and taking advantage of modern tire technology and larger tire sizes. *Hotchkis Sport Suspension*

# EFFECTS OF WHEEL, TIRE, AND SUSPENSION MODIFICATIONS

In some respects a competition package is easier to create than a street package. *Eibach Springs*

## Changing to High Performance Tires, Ultra High Performance Tires, and Wider Tires

**Improves:** Braking performance, acceleration performance, cornering performance

**Problems:** Accelerated tire wear, increased body roll causing more camber change and less cornering traction, increased ride harshness

Rigid lower control arms and frame braces also reduce flex. The larger, stickier tires that are now available from tire companies can easily create enough traction to exceed 1.0 g of cornering force. Lower control arms are vulnerable to flex, especially on older muscle cars. The lower control arms from Hotchkis eliminate flex, and combined with chassis bracing, can really allow suspension tuning that results in high levels of lateral traction. *Hotchkis Sport Suspension*

## Stiffer Suspension Springs

**Improves:** Lower ride height for better handling and looks, reduced body roll for improved tire traction, quicker response to driver steering inputs, improved handling balance if well engineered

**Problems:** Harsher ride, handling balance too extreme if poorly engineered. Cut (shortened) springs or poorly engineered springs can allow suspension or chassis to bottom out, leading to potential damage or crashes

If well engineered, stiffer suspension springs allow lower ride height for better handling and looks, reduced body roll for improved tire traction, quicker response to driver steering inputs, and improved handling balance. *Eibach Springs*

## Stiffer Suspension Anti-roll Bars

**Improves:** Reduced body roll for improved tire traction, quicker response to driver steering inputs, improved handling balance if well engineered

**Problems:** Slightly harsher ride, handling balance too extreme if poorly engineered

Stiffer suspension anti-roll bars reduce body roll for improved tire traction, provide quicker response to driver steering inputs, and improve handling balance—if the system is well engineered. *Progress Technology*

## Stiffer Suspension Bushings

**Improves:** Quicker response to driver steering inputs, less compliance in suspension for improved tire wear and handling

**Problems:** Harsher ride, sometimes noisier

Stiffer suspension bushings provide quicker response to driver steering inputs and less compliance in suspension. This Aurora spherical bearing is solid and virtually eliminates any compliance in the control arm. *Eibach Springs*

## Stiffer Shock Absorber Rates

**Improves:** Quicker response to driver steering inputs, better feel of steering, improved handling during cornering, braking, and acceleration transitions when valving is correct for application

**Problems:** Harsher ride, handling deterioration if incorrectly valved for application

Stiffer shocks provide quicker response to driver steering inputs; better feel of steering; improved handling during cornering, braking, and acceleration transitions—when the valving is correct for the application. *Hotchkis Sport Suspension*

## Competition Packages

In some respects, a competition package is even easier to create than a street package. There are fewer compromises because ride quality is not an issue. However, everything must be perfect. Total tire traction is the most significant goal. Suspension alignment, crossweight, roll couple distribution, suspension frequencies, shock rates and responsiveness must all be perfect to achieve maximum traction.

In all cases, a well-designed system made from quality materials will assure that your goals are realized. Consult with manufacturers or dealers. Web sites and catalogs provide excellent information, and many companies have trained sales staffs to help you with specific applications.

## Suspension Alignment

After making any suspension modifications (as opposed to just wheel/tire changes), have the alignment checked. In most cases, realignment will be required. For street, use factory settings for toe, camber, and caster. For competition, use the component manufacturer's specs, or refer to the alignment chapter in this book.

Camber plates like this one from Eibach allow quick, easy, and accurate camber adjustments in order to assure that the entire tire contact patch is working at maximum traction levels. *Eibach Springs*

These Hotchkis upper control arm brackets are more rigid and also act as bump stops. *Hotchkis Sport Suspension*

Chassis bracing reduces body and chassis flex, making suspension tuning easier and more precise. *Hotchkis Sport Suspension*

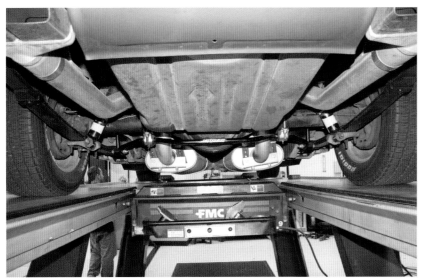

This rear anti-roll bar uses brackets that weld onto the rear axle housing. While this bar is not adjustable, it can easily be swapped for a larger or smaller diameter bar for tuning roll couple distribution and handling balance. *Hotchkis Sport Suspension*

Using adjustable front tie rods with rod ends instead of ball joints allows easy toe-in/out adjustments. They also allow easy bump steer adjustments by placing shims between the rod end and the pitman or steering arms, as seen here on the steering arm near the wheel and tire. *Hotchkis Sport Suspension*

# Chapter 6
# Suspension Components

For a car to achieve good handling, whether on the street or track, the suspension components must be engineered to work together to achieve the optimum compromises both for the type of car and for the use of the car. A pure competition vehicle will have different requirements than a street ride. But a well-conceived suspension system for a street car will work very well on a track day car or for occasional autocrossing. As long as lap time is not an important consideration, a good street suspension package will be great fun on the track or autocross course for the occasionally hot lapping day.

Several key components make up the suspension system, including springs, anti-roll bars, shock absorbers, bushings, and control components, as well as wheels and tires, which will be covered separately. Let's look more closely at the function and purpose of each component.

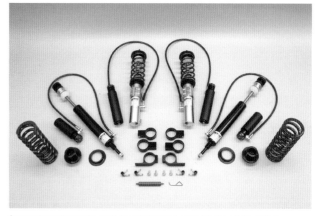

Suspension components must be engineered to work together. *Eibach Springs*

*Progress Technology*

## SPRINGS

The heart of a suspension system is the springs. Springs perform five critical jobs. First, they keep the chassis and suspension from bottoming out over bumps. Second, they control the tires over bumps. Third, they control body roll during cornering, chassis squat during acceleration, and chassis dive under braking. Fourth, the springs determine how the load on the tires shifts during braking, cornering, and acceleration. This is a major factor in establishing the neutral handling balance of the car. And finally, the springs are the major factor in establishing the ride height (ground clearance) of the chassis. If springs are too soft, the chassis or suspension could bottom out over bumps. The body can roll, dive, or squat too much causing the tire contact patch

to be tilted relative to the road surface, hurting traction. If the springs are too stiff, ride quality is unacceptable for street driving and the tire contact patch can lose contact with the road surface over bumps and ruts. The series of compromises needed to create the ideal setup for a given car and performance application require experience, sound engineering, and testing.

Sport springs should lower the car, which not only improves the look but also lowers the center of gravity and improves handling performance. But if the springs are not stiff enough at the lower ground clearance the chassis or suspension will bottom, causing damage to the chassis or suspension. If the springs are too stiff, the ride is horrible and tire contact patch control over bumps deteriorates.

*Progress Technology*

*Eibach Springs*

*Eibach Springs*

Springs are designed to control grip over bumps and ride quality. They should allow the car to be as low as possible without bottom either on the ground or the suspension bump stops. And they need to be soft enough to help keep the tire contact patches loaded on the road or track surface. All other components are designed around the springs.

The red springs on the left are soft. They have a small wire diameter, more coils, and a fairly large overall diameter, all contributing to a softer spring rate. The set of gray springs on the right has fewer coils, thicker wire, and smaller diameter, all contributing to a stiffer spring. *Eibach Springs*

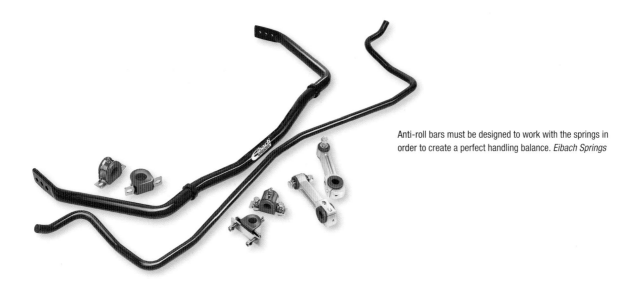

Anti-roll bars must be designed to work with the springs in order to create a perfect handling balance. *Eibach Springs*

For a competition situation, ride comfort is not an issue, but controlling the tire contact patch over bumps is a major concern. Bumpy surfaces require softer springs than smooth surfaces. This compromise is critical.

On the highway, a good set of sport springs, designed and tested for aggressive street applications from a reputable manufacturer, will offer a good compromise between performance and an acceptable ride. Springs designed for racing applications, whether stock replacement springs or coil-over racing springs, will prove to be too stiff for either comfort or tire control over bumps, so that is not the best way to go for street driving. Often ride height is a concern with more aggressive springs. Sticking with a package designed for highway use is the best course to follow.

Spring rates, wheel rates, and suspension frequencies are covered in the vehicle dynamics chapter. We will look more closely at these factors when we discuss suspension tuning.

## ANTI-ROLL BARS

Anti-roll bars are an almost magical invention. They provide an excellent means for adjusting roll couple distribution (handling balance). They also control body roll, thus reducing camber change. This allows the tire contact patch to stay flatter on the road surface during cornering at the traction limit. By doing these two important jobs, anti-roll bars allow the spring rates to do their job of keeping the tire contact patches on the road surface over bumps. Making adjustments to the front and rear anti-roll bars is an excellent way to tune handling balance without affecting ride quality significantly.

### How Anti-roll Bars Work

Anti-roll bars attach to the chassis in bushing mounts. These mounts allow the bar to rotate but hold it firmly in place relative to the chassis. The ends of the anti-roll bar have arms that attach to the suspension with links that allow the free movement of the arms with the suspension. The arms are most often part of the bar which is bent at or near a 90-degree angle to the main section of the bar. Multiple bends are often used for clearance. Some anti-roll bars have detachable arms with splines fitting on splines on the bar itself.

When the bar is twisted, it acts like a spring or torsion bar, providing resistance to the twisting motion. A larger diameter bar resists twisting more and a longer arm on the bar resists twisting less. When a vehicle turns into a corner, weight transfer causes the body to roll. Springs resist body roll, but not enough to control camber change in a high performance or motorsports application. The anti-roll bar adds resistance to body roll, helping to control camber change as well as providing a means of tuning roll couple distribution.

As the body begins to roll, the outside suspension moves into bump travel and the inside suspension moves into rebound travel. This causes the bar to twist, providing resistance to roll. This resistance is not immediate, however. Compliance in the bushings and end links slows the twisting motion. Solid bushings and rod end–style links reduce compliance the most. Polyurethane bushings offer excellent resistance to compliance and are good in most motorsports applications and a good compromise for the street. They offer good responsiveness without too much ride harshness and lower levels of noise and vibration. Rubber bushings have the highest degree of compliance and are not suitable for high performance and motorsports applications.

The downside of anti-roll bars is the connection between left side and right side suspensions. Independent suspension is no longer truly independent with an anti-roll bar. Over two bumps, the anti-roll bar has no effect, but over single wheel bumps, the bar twists, acting like a spring and adding its rate to the wheel rate of the spring. This increases the frequency of the suspension at that corner, and hurts the ability of the suspension to keep the tire contact patch firmly on the road.

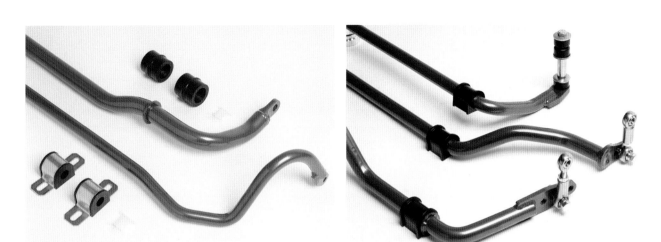

These anti-roll bar packages from Progress Technology show the major difference between bar designs. The bar at left is not adjustable, while the one at right has a bracket for multiple mounting points allowing rate adjustments. *Progress Technology*

Here is a detail shot of an adjustable anti-roll bar mounted on a car. By moving the mounting bolt fore and aft on the bar bracket, the rate of the bar is altered. Lengthening the bar arm (moving the link toward the end) softens the bar while moving it inward stiffens the bar. *Progress Technology*

## Types of Anti-roll Bars

Anti-roll bars can be made of solid bar stock or tubing that is bent into the proper shape with arms at approximately right angles to the chassis-mounted section of the bar. Some racing bars are made of solid or tubular straight sections splined on the end. Arms, usually made of aluminum and also splined, provide the leverage to twist the bar.

## How Anti-roll Bars Influence Handling

Earlier, we discussed roll couple distribution. The combined resistance to body roll provided by the springs and anti-roll bars at the front vs. the rear is the roll couple distribution. Even though anti-roll bars distribute transferred weight differently than springs, the effect is the same. If you stiffen the front anti-roll bar, the understeer is increased (or oversteer decreased). If you stiffen the rear anti-roll bar, the oversteer is increased (or understeer decreased). Softening a bar has the opposite effect.

If a car oversteers during steady state cornering, a softer rear anti-roll bar or a stiffer front anti-roll bar should help reduce or eliminate the condition. Which bar to change depends on several factors covered in the tuning section of this book.

There are situations where increasing the stiffness of an anti-roll bar will have the opposite effect. Most stock vehicles have excessive understeer because it is easier to control and provides more stability for the average driver than a vehicle that oversteers. A big part of this understeer is due to excessive body roll, which induces too much camber change and causes a good portion of the front tire contact patches to lose contact with the road. In this instance, adding a stiffer front anti-roll bar—which should increase the extreme understeer—actually reduces the understeer by reducing the body roll-induced camber change. The front tires now stay in better contact with the road surface, creating more traction and reducing understeer. This is an old trick in SCCA autocrossing in stock classes where few modifications are allowed, but changing the front anti-roll bar is allowed.

On a front drive car with a front weight in excess of 59 percent, the rear bar will be quite stiff. For competition, the bar will be stiff enough to lift the inside rear tire contact patch off the ground slightly in a corner at the limits of traction. For the highway, the bar should be softer for improved stability.

## Anti-roll Bar Pre-load

Most stock anti-roll bars use end links with no vertical adjustment. Most aftermarket anti-roll kits use adjustable end links to eliminate anti-roll bar pre-load. Pre-load means the bar has a twist in it while stationary. Pre-load on an anti-roll bar is undesirable. The reason is that at some point during body roll, a pre-loaded bar will unload for an instant. This will happen in only one direction depending on which way the bar is pre-loaded. For street driving, when the limits

By design, this drift car is oversteering. For fast lap times with the show of drifting, the setup of this car is way off. The rear springs and anti-roll bar are too stiff.

These older racers show the difference between a neutral handling car and one with understeer. The inside car has a perfect setup. The outside car likely has a good setup but could use a stiffer rear bar, or more likely in this case, the driver overdrove the corner entry and induced understeer in the heat of battle.

of tire traction are never reached in cornering, you would never notice the pre-load. In a competition situation at the corner limits of tire traction, the moment the bar unloads, the handling balance will abruptly change. Then, as body roll continues, the bar will again be loaded and again the balance will change. This is both slow and unpleasant. It is very hard to drive smoothly with a pre-loaded bar, at least in one direction.

Pre-load is eliminated by adjusting the end links so that the anti-roll bar is free. This should be done at standard ride height with the driver in place. This is less critical on the highway, but for competition, the driver's weight needs to be in the driver's seat to eliminate pre-load. Disconnect one end link and adjust its length (longer or shorter) until it can easily be reattached without twisting the anti-roll bar.

### Factors Determining Anti-roll Bar Rates

Four factors determine the rate of an anti-roll bar: the diameter of the bar along its active length, the length of the anti-roll bar arms, the active length of the anti-roll bar, and the modulus of elasticity (strength) of the bar material. The effects of changes to the diameter is to the fourth power, a major factor since doubling the bar diameter makes the bar eight times stiffer. The effect of active length is linear, with longer bars having less resistance to twist. The bar arms affect the rate of the anti-roll bar in a linear manner also and a shorter arm increases the anti-roll bar stiffness. The modulus of the material, which is nearly always high tensile strength steel, is considered a constant. Because of multiple bends in a stock replacement anti-roll bar, it is difficult to calculate the rates. Most manufacturers calculate rates rather than check the actual rate of the bar mechanically. Keep in mind that small diameter changes mean big changes in rate, while small changes in arm length mean small changes in rate. Adjustable anti-roll bars have multiple mounts on the arms to change the arm length and therefore the bar rate.

### Anti-roll Bar Motion Ratios

Just like springs, anti-roll bars have motion ratios. The closer the anti-roll bar link is mounted to the centerline of the ball joint the higher the motion ratio. If the ball joint on the control arm moves one inch but the mounting link of the anti-roll bar moves only a half inch, the motion ratio is 0.50. And like the wheel rate of a spring, the motion ratio is squared to determine the bar rate acting at the wheel. The ratio is squared because of the distance difference and the leverage reduction.

### Adjustable Anti-roll Bars

As we have said, the most convenient way to adjust roll couple distribution (handling balance) is by changing anti-roll bar rates. And the easiest way to accomplish that is with an adjustable anti-roll bar. Study the photos of adjustable anti-roll bars to see how they work. To determine how to tune the bar, refer to the previous section on how anti-roll bars affect handling.

Shown here are several mounting methods for adjustable anti-roll bars. The most important criteria is to eliminate any bind and to be able to adjust the anti-roll bar end links (the link connecting the bar to the suspension arm) so that the bar has no pre-load when the car is at rest.
*Progress Technology*

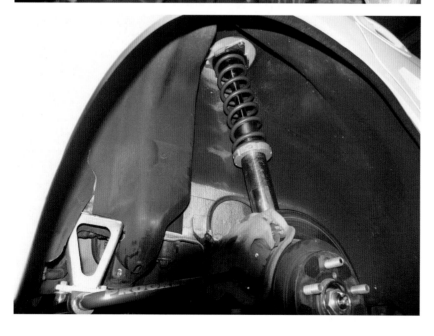

# SHOCKS

## How Shocks Work

Shock absorbers don't actually absorb shocks, but rather dampen vibrations. Shocks are more often called dampers for that reason, but we'll stick with shock absorber as a matter of tradition. When the suspension on a car moves, the shock is designed to control movements of the suspension, working in conjunction with the springs. The springs actually absorb shocks over bumps and control body roll. The shocks control the oscillations of the springs, determining how fast the spring moves up and down. Stiffer shock rates slow spring movements while a softer shock rate allows the spring to move faster. A shock is way too soft if it allows the springs to oscillate, or bounce, more than one full cycle. You've probably driven, or seen, a car with worn shocks bouncing down the road after hitting a bump. A shock is way too stiff if the shock limits spring travel. A shock that is too stiff can cause the tire contact patch to bounce off the road surface over bumps or jack weight in the car after body roll occurs.

## Bumps

The first job of a shock is to control the tire contact patch over bumps. In racing, a shock that is too soft allows the chassis to bounce after hitting a bump or rut. The car feels like it wallows. If the shock is too stiff, when a bump is encountered the tire contact patch can be pulled off the track surface, or at least the load on that tire is reduced significantly. This affects handling balance and jack weights around the chassis, making the car feel unpredictable. The loss of traction is considerable and the car is very hard for the driver to read. Over bumps, the car feels like it skates.

This cutaway of a shock shows some of the valving and the shaft of the shock. *Progress Technology*

While difficult to see, this car just hit a bump on the track and the right rear tire is off the ground slightly. This is an indication that the bump valving on this shock is too stiff combined with a spring which is also too stiff. *Progress Technology*

The coil-over unit consists of the shock and the spring. The body of the shock is threaded (or a threaded collar slips over the shock) for a spring perch. This allows ride height adjustments for ground clearance and to set ride heights for adjusting crossweight percentages. *Progress Technology*

The coil-over kit shown in the middle is for a strut suspension. The end link with spherical bearing is for the anti-roll bar mount. The spring on the left has a threaded collar and an adjustable perch for adjusting ride height. The perch and collar slide over a bare shock (top) and the perch is supported by a snap ring in a groove around the shock body. *Progress Technology*

A shock dampens vibrations by creating friction. Racing shocks all use hydraulic fluid in a tube with a piston. The piston pushes the fluid through a series of valves and bleeds, controlling the "rate" of the shock. The valves and bleed can be varied to change the rate. Different valves and bleeds are used for rebound and compression and different valves are used for different shaft speeds. The valves for either rebound or compression at various shaft speeds can be changed, together or independently, to change how the shock valving works over bumps or during body roll and pitch under braking and acceleration.

In general terms, different shaft speeds come into play for different jobs. Slow shaft speeds occur during roll and pitch. The valving for slow shaft speed has the greatest effect on transitional handling, and when a shock is adjustable, it is usually the low speed valving that can be altered. High shaft speeds come into play over bumps and ruts and affect the control of the tire contact patch over bumps and ruts. Medium shaft speeds have an influence over both handling and bumps.

There are several types of shock designs, but all have the same effect on the chassis. Some shocks are gas charged and some are not. The differences are mostly in design, performance as heat builds up, wear, reliability, and rebuilding potential.

## Bump vs. Rebound

Bump, or compression, occurs when the shock shaft is being moved into the body. This occurs on the front of a bump, the back of a rut, the right side when turning left, the left side shocks when exiting a left turn, the front under braking, and the rear under acceleration.

Rebound, or extension, occurs when the shaft is being pulled from the body. This occurs on the backside of a bump, the front of a rut, the left side shocks in a left turn, the right side shocks exiting a left turn, the front under acceleration, and the rear under braking.

## Shaft Speeds

How fast the shock moves affects the rate of the shock in both bump and rebound. Shocks are speed sensitive, with speed referring to the speed of the shaft movement in and out of the shock body. Different shaft speeds use different valves for controlling the rate or force of the shock. Shocks work mostly within a range of about 3 inches/second to about 20 inches/second. The lower speeds come into play during weight transfer when the body is rolling or pitching. The higher speeds come into play over bumps and ruts. A shock manufacturer can alter low, medium, and high speed valving to control what the shock does in different situations. Low and medium speed valving are used to control how the shock influences handling.

For best braking performance when braking into a corner, you want weight to transfer quickly onto the front tires. Stiffer bump rates in the front and stiffer rebound rates at the rear can help accomplish this regardless of the platform—front-drive, AWD, or rear-drive. *Progress Technology*

When exiting a turn, it is desirable to get weight transferred on to the drive wheels as quickly as possible on a rear drive car, or to keep weight on the front tires as long as possible, like the front drive car in the photo. In the case of a front-drive car, softer rebound valving in the front and softer bump valving in the rear will help.
*Progress Technology*

## How Shocks Affect Weight Transfer

There are four components to weight transfer:

1. **How Much Weight Is Transferred**
   This is influenced by the weight of the car, the track width/wheelbase, the center of gravity height, and the cornering force.
2. **Where Weight Is Transferred**
   This is influenced by the spring rates acting at the tire contact patch, the anti-roll bar rates, and some lateral locating bars on rear suspensions.
3. **When Weight Is Transferred**
   This is influenced by when the driver uses the controls: the steering, the brakes, and accelerator.
4. **How Fast Weight Is Transferred**
   This is influenced by the shock rates and by how quickly the driver uses the controls.

## How Shocks Affect Handling

The low- and medium-speed valving of the shock controls how fast weight is transferred. This affects the load on a tire and can change the handling balance while weight is being transferred. Once all weight has been transferred, the shock no longer influences handling. Since weight is almost always being transferred, the shocks are almost always affecting handling balance.

In general, rebound damping controls how fast weight leaves a tire while bump controls how fast weight goes onto a tire. Stiffer valving causes a shock to react more quickly; softer valving slows the reaction of the shock. Stiffer valving gets the load to change more quickly. Stiffer rebound valving gets the load off a tire more quickly and onto an opposite tire faster. Stiffer bump valving gets the load onto that tire faster.

If all the valving—both bump and rebound at all four corners—are changed equally, the effect of handling balance is nothing. If only bump or rebound is changed, then there is an effect. If only one end or one corner is changed, there is also an effect. We will look more closely at this in a later chapter.

## How the Driver Affects What the Shocks Do

The driver affects what the shocks do by how fast the driver uses the controls. For example very fast steering wheel movements cause the body to roll faster and change the shaft speed of the shocks. This changes the rate of the shock and affects handling by changing the rate of weight transfer. This can be compounded by the fact that the driver is most often using more than one control at a time. How fast the driver turns the steering wheel and how fast the driver pushes on the brake pedal has a big effect on the handling going into a corner. It is for this reason that the driver must be really smooth when using the controls. Abrupt steering or pedal applications can affect the handling in a negative way, and it can be very tough to tune the chassis to overcome this.

## Split-Valve and Adjustable Shocks

Split-valve shocks are built with different valving in either bump or rebound from what is normal for a specific shock. This allows chassis tuning for fine-tuning specific handling problems by changing one or more shocks. Adjustable shocks can offer adjustments in rebound only, or for both bump and rebound (double adjustable). Tuning can be accomplished by adjusting the shock absorber, most often while still on the car. In any case, changing the valving of shocks overall, in bump only or rebound only, can change the handling of the car and improve lap times. For the most part, tuning with shocks is considered a fine-tuning adjustment once the chassis is set up and tuned.

## SHOCK ABSORBER TIPS

### Travel

Shock travel is very important. The more travel from a shock, the better it can do its job. When a car is lowered and retains stock shocks, travel in bump is often reduced, even eliminated. This can cause damage to the shock or strut and even create a serious handling problem that could cause a loss of control. When a car is lowered, shocks should be part of a coordinated suspension package to provide adequate suspension travel and improved performance.

For racing, shocks should be mounted as close to the ball joint on a front lower control arm as possible, and as close to the hub on the rear axle; but do not compromise clearance with components, and on the front, check clearance during full steering travel.

### Bottoming Out

If a shock bottoms or reaches full extension under load, damage can occur. Bump stops on the shaft of the shocks reduce this and some shock or strut manufacturers use rebound travel limiters to keep the shock from reaching full extension. Full extension is usually less of a problem.

### Cooling

Shocks dampen by using friction, which causes heat. Heat buildup can affect the rate of the shock, always softening it. Dissipating heat always helps shock performance. Bumpy tracks create more heat than smooth. It is best not to cover shocks, and even to duct cool air to the shocks. Aluminum shocks dissipate heat faster than steel bodies. For coil-overs, threaded body shocks cool better than smooth body shocks with thread spring perches over the body for the coil-over adjusters.

### Checking Shocks

Shocks should be checked regularly for binds and pitting in the shafts. It is a good idea to check for dead spots by extending the shock fully and putting a sudden load on the shock by hand. Do the same with the shock fully compressed and pull in the shaft abruptly. A dead spot will be obvious, and that shock needs to be rebuilt or replaced.

### Dyno Testing Shocks

Dyno testing a shock gives the owner exact data on the bump and rebound rates at several shaft speeds. Once a combination is found to work, that combination can be repeated if and when a shock needs to be rebuilt or replaced. You can also tell if a shock is worn—and how much it is worn—by testing it on a shock dyno.

## Rebuilding Shocks

Some shocks can be easily rebuilt, and it is usually much cheaper to have a shock rebuilt than to buy a new one. In general, steel body shocks from most manufacturers cannot be rebuilt while many aluminum body shocks can be rebuilt. Check with your dealer or shock manufacturer.

## BUSHINGS, CAMBER ADJUSTERS, CHASSIS BRACES

A wide variety of components are manufactured to enhance the handling performance of cars in both street and motorsports applications. Some of these products allow easier, quicker, and more accurate suspension adjustments, enabling improved performance. Other products reduce compliance and flex in the suspension and chassis, allowing improved responsiveness to driver control inputs and better performance. The flip side of these products is the increase in noise and ride harshness in varying degrees depending upon the nature and design of the product. For vehicles used only in competition, noise and harshness are not issues. For the street, some excellent compromises exist, allowing significant performance and response improvements without excessive increases in noise and harshness. Let's look at these product categories in more detail.

### Suspension Bushings

Suspension bushings are used to mount suspension components to the chassis of a vehicle. Rubber and other compliant materials are used in stock vehicles to isolate road noise and ride harshness from passengers. Race cars use solid metal or other rigid materials to reduce compliance and improve responsiveness with no consideration to comfort. Solid, rigid bushings are sometimes used on the street, but the road noise and harshness become uncomfortable even for the most die-hard performance enthusiast.

The best compromise for street vehicles and even cars used for both highway and motorsports applications is urethane bushings. They are quite rigid, but maintain reasonable noise levels and offer just enough compliance to keep your teeth from rattling out on bumpy roads and interstate highways. And urethane bushings are available for many, if not most, street applications.

For every soft bushing you replace in the suspension system, responsiveness and performance will improve. Polyurethane is used in suspensions for shock absorber bushings, suspension bump stops, radius/strut arm bushings, coil spring isolators, damper donuts, leaf spring pads, torque arm bushings, and rack and pinion bushings.

### Other Bushings and Mounts

As with the suspension systems, other mounts and bushings are available for the driveline, including the engine and transmission. Mounts are also available for the body. The most readily available bushings and mounts are made from polyurethane. Polyurethane motor and transmission mounts will isolate vibrations, but greatly reduce compliance and mount twisting under the torque loads of acceleration and braking. Replacing stock rubber mounts and bushings for any form of competition or combination street/competition vehicle is very desirable from a performance, wear/reliability, and safety standpoint. Even with stock horsepower, today's ultra high performance and race compound DOT tires make so much traction that damage to motor and transmission mounts can occur during hard acceleration (especially launches), and limit braking. Stiffer, stronger bushings and mounts will eliminate the problem of stock rubber parts and improve performance.

This anti-roll bar kit uses polyurethane bushings, which are stiffer than stock, but retain some compliance and are quieter for good performance on the street. *Eibach Springs*

The stock rubber bushings are visible in this photo. Stock bushings are quiet and comfortable, but have too much compliance for high performance applications. *Progress Technology*

### Strut and Chassis Braces

A wide variety of strut tower braces and chassis stiffeners are available for a wide range of vehicle applications. The worst form of compliance in a vehicle is chassis/body flex. When the chassis flexes, not only is performance and responsiveness hurt, but the chassis becomes a very large undampened spring which is nearly impossible to tune. This flex also causes premature wear to the chassis structure. Many of today's vehicles lack sufficient chassis rigidity for performance and motorsports applications. While they perform just fine in normal driving situations, the addition of stiffer suspension components, sticky, low profile tires, and harder bushings and mounts increases chassis flex to much higher degrees. The flex robs performance.

A wide range of bolt-on strut tower braces and other chassis stiffeners are readily available. The addition of these products will greatly reduce chassis flex and improve performance. The addition of a roll bar or especially a roll cage will add even more chassis rigidity to a vehicle for any motorsports activity. The increase in driver safety is also a major plus for roll bars and roll cages.

### Camber Adjusters

While many cars have some form of camber adjustment built into the front suspension and fewer have rear camber adjustments, most are cumbersome and time-consuming. Being able to quickly and accurately adjust camber is important for high performance applications and crucial for motorsports. A convenient camber adjustment for dual purpose cars allows different settings for the street and for competition.

The most common camber adjuster is the camber plate made primarily for strut-equipped vehicles. Other types of camber adjusters include spacers, adjustable "A" arms, and eccentric bushings.

## SPHERICAL BEARINGS/ROD ENDS

The ultimate way to eliminate compliance and improve responsiveness in a competition car is the use of spherical bearings and rod ends throughout the suspension system. These bearings are very rigid and allow angular movement with very little free play. They also transmit vibration and noise very effectively, making them less than desirable for any street application.

Eccentric suspension bushings can be used to adjust camber. *Progress Technology*

Special ball joints and upper control arms allow both camber and caster adjustments. *Eibach Springs*

## PANHARD BARS AND LATERAL LOCATING DEVICES

On solid axle vehicles, like most rear axles on older American vehicles and some front-wheel drive cars, some means of lateral location of the axle is needed. In most cases, a Panhard bar is used. Other devices include the Watt's linkage and the Jacob's ladder. In all cases, the devices allow free vertical movement but eliminate lateral movement of the axle. The Panhard bar is most often used. On stock applications, they use rubber bushings which allow compliance and considerable lateral displacement during cornering at the limits of traction, especially with sticky tires and modified suspension. Solid bushings or rod ends on competition cars and polyurethane bushings for the street will eliminate or minimize the compliance.

## DRAG STRUTS

Some vehicles use drag struts on the front suspension, usually as part of the lower control arm. Drag struts are often adjustable, allowing an easy and quick means of adjusting caster. Aftermarket adjustable drag struts are available for some applications. Unless flex is an issue, aftermarket drag struts will offer little in performance gains, but the added convenience of caster adjustment is worth considering.

Spherical bearings and solid metal bushings can be used on suspension control arms to reduce compliance on track-only cars. On the street, the ride harshness and noise would be unacceptable for most people. *Progress Technology*

Rod ends with spherical bearings work great for suspension and steering components where length adjustments are useful, like upper control arms and steering tie rods. *Progress Technology*

Panhard bars are used to locate solid axles laterally. Adjustable rod ends allow easy alignment. On a race car, rod ends with spherical bearings are important to make sure that the axle is unable to move from side to side. *Progress Technology*

## SUSPENSION CONTROL ARMS

Many companies make suspension control arms, both upper and lower "A" arms for front suspension and trailing arms for the rear suspension depending upon the application. In most cases, these aftermarket arms are stronger and often lighter than the stock components. Reducing weight of suspension components reduces unsprung weight, which improves control of the tire contact patch over bumps. In some cases, the aftermarket arms are adjustable where the original equipment arms are not. Adjustability allows fine-tuning of suspension settings for improved performance.

## LIMITED SLIP DIFFERENTIALS

A standard differential allows the drive wheels to rotate at different speeds so that drag is reduced while cornering. This is a good thing if acceleration is not an issue. If you are reading this book, chances are acceleration is a big issue with you. The stock differential directs torque to the least loaded tire,

allowing wheelspin to occur earlier than is desirable. This is a big issue when launching a car from a standing start in drag racing or autocrossing. It is also an issue exiting slow and medium speed corners when the inside tire is still unloaded and can easily spin when the regular differential directs more torque to the unloaded tire. This is obviously worse with more power, but a front driver has a bigger problem than a rear driver because weight transfer during acceleration is off of the front tires.

Many oval track cars use a spool to lock the left and right rear drive wheels together. This creates high cornering drag, but helps with acceleration off the turns. This is less than desirable for road racing, autocrossing, or drag racing, and plain dangerous for the highway. The best solution is a limited slip differential that transmits more torque to the tire with more traction, but still allows a high degree of freewheeling during cornering. This reduces drag but greatly improves traction during launches and corner exits.

Some custom A-arms use slotted attachment points on the chassis for camber adjustments. *Progress Technology*

There are several types of limited slip differentials. Many performance vehicles are equipped with them from the factory, and several brands are available for competition. Some are adjustable, allowing earlier lock-up of the differential clutches. In most cases, they greatly enhance performance. If one drive wheel is spinning easily on your car, consider a limited slip differential.

## REVIEW

It is important to remember that each component in the suspension system has a primary function. Using a different component to do the job of another component is both undesirable for performance as well as potentially dangerous. The prime example is using stiffer springs to control body roll. The springs are then too stiff to do their job of keeping the tire contact patches on the road surface. The entire system must be properly engineered for the application and intended use, especially for motorsports. Varying from this approach can reduce performance but can also create a dangerous situation by deteriorating handling under certain conditions instead of improving it.

The A-arm above has adjusting slots built in to adjust both camber and caster; the A-arm below uses a simple slot for the ball joint. *Eibach Springs*

Every component of the suspension system must be engineered and tested for the specific application. *Eibach Springs*

# Chapter 7
# Vehicle Preparation and Setup

After selecting and installing a suspension system, it's time to get the suspension set up. For highway-only use, a good alignment is necessary, and unless you have the equipment and experience, you are better off going to an alignment shop. If you plan to get on the racetrack with your ride, then there are a few more setup procedures that will assure maximum performance and improved reliability. These procedures become even more important if you are competing for time, such as a time attack or autocross event.

## SUSPENSION ALIGNMENT

You just spent $3,000 on wheels, tires, sport springs, and shocks. With great anticipation, you take your car out on your favorite canyon road for the first time after installing the new parts. While the car feels very stiff and responsive, the handling improvement is not what you anticipated and you feel very disappointed.

This is very common, but often there is a simple cure for the problem. In virtually every case, the suspension needs to be aligned after installing a suspension package. Lowering a car especially causes camber and toe settings to change and often caster is also changed. For most people, using a good alignment shop that understands high performance suspensions is the easiest way to get your car back to proper alignment settings. If you prefer to do it yourself, follow the procedures and use the settings found in the factory repair manual for your vehicle.

For most street applications, using the factory camber, toe, and caster settings is best. We'll look at the effects of changes for each specific setting later. For competition, different settings will offer improved performance on the track, but these settings could result in excessive tire wear for street driving; straight line stability could be compromised if you are using settings ideal for the racetrack or autocross course. Let's examine each of the specific settings that require attention.

*Eibach Springs*

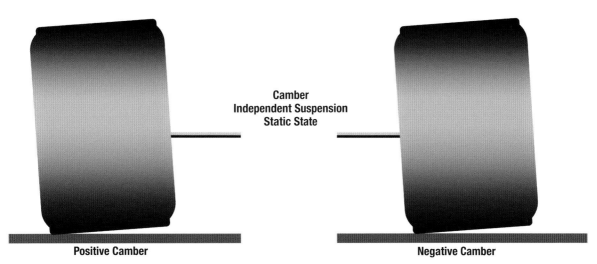

**Camber**
**Independent Suspension**
**Static State**

**Positive Camber**   **Negative Camber**

Camber is the tilt of the tire when viewed from the front. Positive camber means the top of the tire is tilted out from the center of the car. Negative camber means the top of the tire is tilted in.

## Setting Camber

As briefly explained in chapter 2, camber is the tilt of the tire when viewed from the front. Positive camber means the top of the tire is tilted out from the center of the car. Negative camber means the top of the tire is tilted in. Camber angles should be measured on all wheels, though with solid rear axle systems camber cannot be adjusted. But many independent rear suspension cars can be adjusted easily. The fact is that camber change nearly always causes

an increase in positive camber, and some static negative camber is beneficial for maximum cornering traction. The downside of this is increased tire wear on the inside edge of the tread. For this reason, on the street, using more than one-half degree negative camber is not good idea. For competition, up to three degrees is acceptable, but greater angles will cause a reduction in straight line braking performance and acceleration, especially launches in drag racing and autocrossing.

These photos show negative camber (above) and positive camber (below). *Hotchkis Sport Suspension*

Camber can be set by an alignment shop, but be sure the place you go to understands high performance suspensions and how you plan to use your car. Having the computer readout provides great accuracy. *Hotchkis Sport Suspension*

Most factory specifications for camber indicate an angle of zero to one-half degree positive. For street performance improvements, use up to one-half degree negative camber.

For motorsports applications, the best way to set camber is to monitor tire temperatures (see chapter 4). The goal is to have nearly equal temperatures across the surface of the tire, with the inside edge of the tire about 5 to 10 degrees F hotter. This indicates the perfect camber angle for your application and track conditions.

To set camber, refer to the factory repair manual for your vehicle or the instructions for aftermarket camber adjusting products. A bubble caster/camber gauge is a good tool, but an electronic gauge is the best tool for setting camber. The key is to use tire temperatures to tune, and then measure the camber angle so that the settings can be repeated.

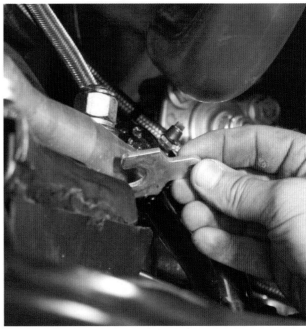

Shims are used to adjust camber angles. *Hotchkis Sport Suspension*

This caster/camber gauge from Eibach provides an accurate and portable way to check camber and caster at the track or in your garage. *Eibach Springs*

Portable camber gauges provide the best way to set camber angles if you are taking your car to the track. *Hotchkis Sport Suspension*

## Setting Caster

Caster is the inclination of the steering axis in the front when viewed from the side. See the diagrams for a better idea of caster angles. Caster adds stability to the steering, and if it's off, either steering effort increases too much or the car looses stability and wanders, especially on grooved interstate highways and on longitudinal expansion strips.

For this reason, caster should always be set to factory specs for the highway, and should never vary more than one degree in either direction for motorsports applications using stock control arms and spindles. An electronic or bubble caster gauge is the best tool to use for setting caster. To set caster, refer to the factory repair manual for your vehicle.

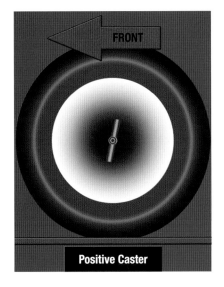

**Positive Caster**

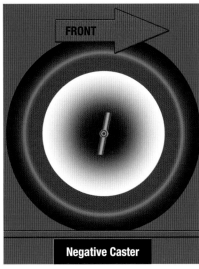

**Negative Caster**

Positive caster is present when the steering pivot, or spindle, is tilted with the top (upper ball joint) behind the vertical centerline of the wheel.

Negative caster is present when the steering pivot, or spindle, is tilted with the top (upper ball joint) in front of the vertical centerline of the wheel.

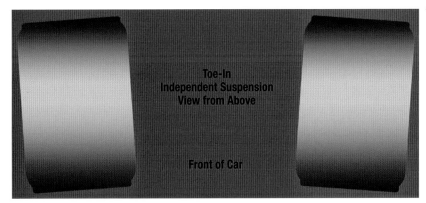

**Toe-In
Independent Suspension
View from Above**

**Front of Car**

Toe-in and toe-out.

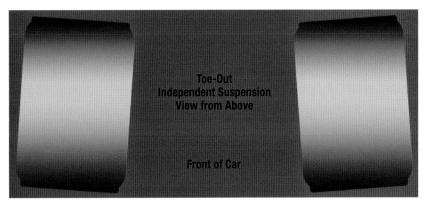

**Toe-Out
Independent Suspension
View from Above**

**Front of Car**

## Setting Toe

Toe is the angle of the front or rear tires relative to each other, side to side, when viewed from above. Toe-in is present when the front edges of the tires are closer together than the rear edges. The opposite is toe-out. Both front and rear should be checked for toe. Most cars need a small amount of rear toe-in for straight line stability. Most manufacturers spec toe-in at the front as well for better steering feel. For motorsports applications, toe-out is usually better for steering response at corner turn-in.

Toe is usually measured in inches or millimeters at the edge of the wheel rim or on the tire tread. The amount of toe is the difference between front and rear measurements either at the rim or on the exact same line on a tire, like a tread groove or line scribed on both tires. If the forward measurement is larger, toe-out is present. The adjustments are made by lengthening or shortening the tie rods. It is best to make half the adjustment at each tie rod when possible, rather than a single large adjustment on one tie rod. Altering tie rod lengths can cause the steering wheel to rotate off center. The absolute best way to measure toe is with a laser toe gauge, especially for motorsports. Other methods are outlined later in this chapter.

For the highway, use factory toe specs front and rear. For motorsports, a small degree of toe-out can be used in the front. The amount depends upon how tight the turns are. More toe-out is effective on a tight autocross course, but less would be used on a fast road course. On the rear, unless the factory specs for your vehicle say otherwise, toe-in should be used.

## Toe Recommendations

All measurements here are in inches and measured at the rim face, which is 15 to 18 inches. If you measure at the tire tread, which is a larger diameter than the rim, use a slightly larger number, about 1/32 inch to 1/16 inch more. For rear suspension with toe adjustments, toe should be about 1/8 inch. More will cause tire drag, which reduces performance and increases tire wear.

For front suspensions, use 1/16 inch to 1/8 inch toe-out for road courses, rallying and import drag front drive cars. For autocrossing, use 1/8 inch to 1/4 inch. If you drive your vehicle to the track, reset the toe for competition and return to factory specs for highway driving to reduce wear and improve stability on the highway. Front drive cars often respond favorably to more front toe-out than rear-drive cars. In any case, be conservative with toe settings.

## Rear Axle Alignment

If your vehicle has adjustable camber and/or toe, follow the above suggestions and refer to your factory repair manual for procedures. If you have a solid rear axle, measure camber and toe. Up to a 1/4 degree per side of negative camber is acceptable, and up to 1/8 inch total toe-in is acceptable. Greater amounts or any toe-out or positive camber will cause problems and the axle should be straightened by an experienced body shop or race car fabricator.

Laser alignment racks with wheel turntables allow quick and accurate toe-setting adjustments. *Hotchkis Sport Suspension*

Lengthening and shortening the tie-rods facilitates toe-in/out adjustments. Using a link or a tie rod with left and right hand threaded tie rod ends will allow easy, quick, and accurate adjustments. This link on a Hotchkis-equipped car has flats milled into the rod so an open end wrench can be used for adjustments. Jam nuts lock the rod in place when finished. *Hotchkis Sport Suspension*

## BUMP STEER

Bump steer, as the name implies, is steering input over bumps due to toe setting changes during suspension travel. The effect is most obvious when you drive over a one-wheel bump and the steering pulls to one side. Bump steer is caused by a conflict between steering geometry and suspension geometry. If you plot the path of the front suspension in bump and rebound travel, and plot the path of the tie rods during travel, they should be identical for zero bump steer.

Often when a car is lowered, the geometry between the suspension and the tie rods changes, causing some bump steer. If this happens, the steering wheel will pull over bumps while going straight. This is usually minor and not a serious concern on the highway. But if the wheel jerks hard over one-wheel bumps, then the problem should be addressed. For motorsports, bump steer, when present, should be eliminated because it causes tire scrub over bumps and reduces straight line speed and hurts cornering performance at the limits of tire adhesion.

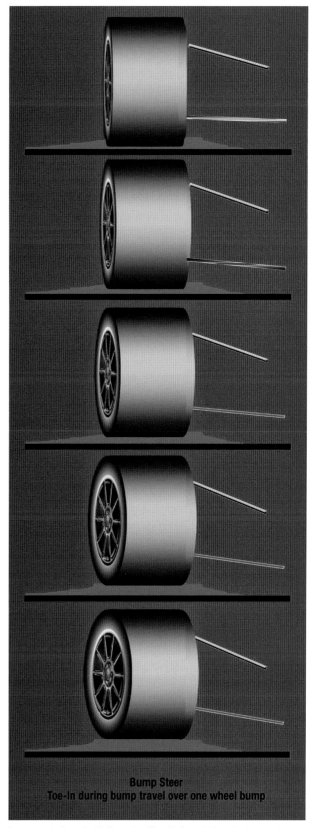

**Bump Steer**
**Toe-In during bump travel over one wheel bump**

Bump steer is shown in this illustration. Here the front tire is toeing in over a bump. This is not caused by turning the steering wheel, but is caused by a disparity between suspension and steering geometry. The effect is exaggerated here.

Measuring bump steer requires measuring toe at various points in bump and rebound travel. To measure bump steer requires the removal of the springs and shocks (just springs on a strut suspension) so that the suspension can be moved easily through bump and rebound travel. Normally, toe is measured at ride height and again at one inch and two inches of both bump and rebound travel. If there is any difference in toe measurements from ride height during bump and/or rebound travel, then bump steer is present. Up to a change of ⅛ inch at two inches of travel is a minor concern for street only vehicles. For competition vehicle, any bump steer should be eliminated.

There are so many different bump steer scenarios that space prohibits addressing ways to cure the condition. It is also very time consuming and often requires fabrication and machining. It is best to find an experienced race preparation shop to cure any bump steer problems.

## ROLL STEER

Roll steer at the rear end is like bump steer in the front. If the toe setting changes during bump and/or rebound travel at the rear, then roll steer is present. Roll steer is less likely than bump steer when a vehicle is lowered. It is measured the same way as bump steer, and is equally difficult to correct.

## WEIGHING, CROSSWEIGHT, AND TUNING WITH CROSSWEIGHT

The weight of a car is a key factor to its performance. While less of an issue for street cars, getting a competition vehicle to the lowest possible weight—at least the lowest weight allowed by the rules—is paramount to success. But just as important is the weight distribution of a car. Getting the weight where it does the most good, or has the least ill effect, is also crucial to performance. While not a high priority on a street car, it is a very high priority for a competition vehicle, even one used on the street as its primary function. While most of this chapter has its primary application for competition, to achieve the highest degree of performance for a street car, the same principles apply.

## THE IMPORTANCE OF WEIGHT DISTRIBUTION

Your car is really fast in right-hand turns, but understeers in left turns. If you get the car neutral in left turns, it oversteers in right turns. The situation is frustrating. You've tried springs, shocks, different bars, neutralizing the anti-roll bar and nothing seems to work. Even on a track with mostly right-hand turns, the problem in the left-hand turns cost a lot of time.

While several different setup parameters could have caused this situation, a likely cause is excessive crossweight. One of the most important aspects of car setup is the static weight distribution and the crossweight percentage. It is important to weigh your car, and find the four individual corner weights. The most effective way to do this is with

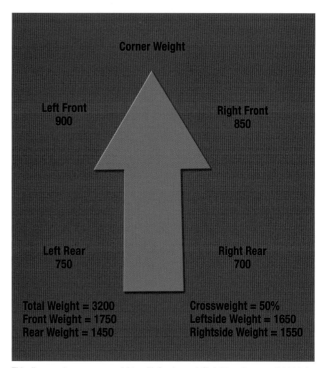

This diagram shows corner weights with front, rear, left, right, and crossweight totals.

electronic corner weight scales, whether you purchase them or borrow them. You can also use public scales by placing one wheel at a time on the weighing platform. However you get the information, the data is important to obtain and understanding how to use the data is even more critical.

## STATIC WEIGHT DISTRIBUTION

Static weight distribution is the weight resting on each tire contact patch with the car at rest exactly the way it will be driven. This means the driver should be in the car, all fluids topped up and the fuel load should be such that, for competition, the car meets your association's minimum weight rule at the designated time, usually after an event. The car should be at minimum weight, using ballast as needed to make the proper weight.

When working with static weight distribution, we use two percentages to analyze the car's corner weights. Left-side weight percent and rear weight percent tell us all we need to know about the setup relative to the weight distribution. The left-side weight percentage is found by adding the left-front weight to the left-rear weight and dividing the sum by the total weight. The rear weight percentage is found in the same way. Add the left-rear and the right-rear weight together and divide the sum by the total weight. Many electronic scales will perform the calculations for you.

For road racing and autocrossing, the ideal left-side weight percentage is 50 percent. This makes the cornering force balanced from left to right and offers the best performance overall. Many cars cannot make the 50-percent left-side weight percentage due to driver offset. It is a worthwhile goal to strive for, though. Rear weight percentage for road racing and autocrossing is less definite. The more power a car has, the more static weight over the drive wheels—up to a point—helps acceleration off the corners. Additionally, it is much more difficult to change rear percentage much, since rear weight is mostly a design function. It still pays to be thoughtful about weight placement fore and aft in your car.

The only way to change the static weight distribution percentages is to physically move weight around in the car. Jacking weight by changing ride heights will not alter the left side or the rear percentages.

## CROSSWEIGHT PERCENTAGE

Crossweight percentage compares the diagonal weight totals to the total car weight. To calculate crossweight percentage, add the right-front weight to the left-rear weight and divide the sum by the total weight of the car. Crossweight is also called wedge. If the percentage is over 50 percent, the car has wedge; below 50 percent the car has reverse wedge. More wedge means that the car will likely understeer more in a left turn. The advantage to wedge on an oval track is that the left (inside) rear tire carries more load, so the car drives off

the turns better. But in a right turn, the opposite occurs and the handling is worse. In almost all cases, the loss of cornering performance in one direction is greater than the gain in the other direction. The optimum crossweight percentage for road racing, time attack, track days, and autocrossing is a very narrow range at 50 percent crossweight. The range is within one-half percent, or 49.5 percent to 50.5 percent.

On oval track cars, crossweight is usually used in conjunction with stagger (where the right-rear tire is larger in circumference than the left-rear tire) to balance handling. More stagger usually loosens the handling (increases oversteer) in left turns, so more crossweight is used to tighten the handling up. But stagger is not a good idea on a road course or autocross either, so the key is 50 percent crossweight and no stagger.

One of the problems with crossweight is that it will change the handling balance from a left to a right turn. This can make maneuvering in traffic difficult, even dangerous. On a road course, the crossweight percentage should be very close to 50 percent, within a half a degree either way, to keep the handling balance similar in a right-hand turn compared to a left-hand turn. In the example at the beginning of this chapter, this was the problem—a crossweight percentage less than 50 percent, probably off by at least 2 percent. One of the keys to a good setup is using the correct procedure to weigh your race car.

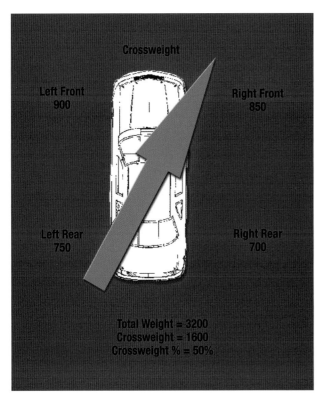

This diagram shows crossweight. Crossweight is found by adding the left rear/right front diagonal total weight and dividing by the total weight of the car with driver in place. For turning corners both directions, 50 percent crossweight is ideal, with no more than a 0.5 percent variation.

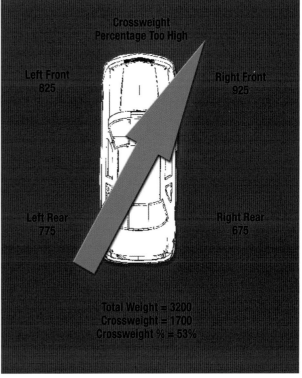

This diagram shows crossweights with too high a percentage for turning left and right. This would be a good oval setup for just left turns. Ideal crossweight totals are 49.5 percent to 50.5 percent.

## HOW TO WEIGH YOUR RACE CAR

Here are some points to remember when weighing your race car.

- Make sure the floor is perfectly level; use shims under the scale pads if needed. Small angles can throw off your readings significantly.
- Set tire pressures first.
- Check stagger at each tire, even with radials for road racing and autocrossing.
- Put the driver weight in the car, preferably the driver.
- Use a load of fuel for where you want the car balanced, either at the start of race, the end of the race, or an average between the two.
- Disconnect the shocks, when possible, and the anti-roll bars.
- Use blocks the same height as your scale pads to move the car off the scales to make adjustments.
- Bounce the car at each corner to free the suspension from any bind, then roll the car on the scales.

- Make sure the tires are centered on the scales.
- Recheck air pressure often to assure ride heights stay consistent.
- Set static weight distribution.
- Check static weight before working on crossweight.
- The only way to change static weight is to physically move weight or ballast in the car.
- To increase left side weight, move weight as far to the left as possible.
- To increase rear weight, move weight as far back as possible.
- Move ballast first, since it's easier; after that you will have to move components like the battery or fuel cell.
- It is best to get 50 percent left side weight percent when possible.
- Get the rear percentage close to 50 percent for rear drive cars and close to 40 percent for front drive cars. Too much front weight can cause the car to become very unstable at speed, a problem for front drive drag race cars.

Electronic corner weight scales are the best tools you can use to weigh your track car.

Make sure that all of the scale pads are level before weighing.

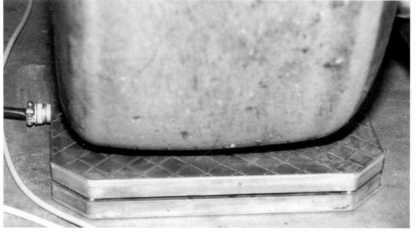

Make sure the tire is centered on the scale pad both fore and aft as well as front to rear. All four tires need to be centered and level. Make sure tire pressures are set to what you use on the track.

# SETTING CROSSWEIGHT

The weight on each corner of the car has an effect on handling. Crossweight—that is, the comparison of the weight resting on diagonal pairs of tires—determines the handling balance in left vs. right turns. Unless they are equal, the car will handle differently turning left as opposed to turning right. Adjusting this so that the diagonal weights are equal will allow the car to handle the same in left vs. right turns. This is done by changing the ride heights of the chassis at each corner of the car. By changing one ride height, the crossweight is altered. This is similar to shortening or lengthening one leg of a chair or table. More weight is forced to rest on the other legs. The most weight rests on the longest leg. On a car, raising the ride height on a corner of the car forces more static weight on that corner. It also puts more weight on the diagonally opposite corner and removes weight from the two other corners. Lowering a ride height takes weight away from that corner and the diagonally opposite corner and adds weight to the two remaining corners. By carefully adjusting ride heights, the ideal crossweight percentage can be obtained. For road racing, time attack, autocrossing, time trials, track days, and rallying, 50 percent crossweight is ideal. Anything outside of 49.5 percent to 50.5 percent will adversely affect handling in one direction while helping in the other. As we have seen in the tire traction chapter, the loss in one direction due to the nature of traction relative to vertical loads on the tire will be too great to be made up for in the other direction. For drag racing, it is still ideal to have the crossweights at 50 percent for straight line stability and optimum launch, but is very important to set the crossweights so that the drive wheels have equal weights in the static state, and the crossweight is as close to 50 percent as possible. This makes a big difference in traction, especially at the launch. Following are some tips for setting crossweights.

- Once static weight percentages are set, work on crossweight percentages.
- You cannot change the left or rear percentages by jacking weight around in the car, but this will change crossweight.
- Changing the ride height at any corner will change the crossweight percentage.
- If you raise the ride height at a given corner (put a turn in or add a round of wedge), the weight on that corner will increase, as will the weight on the diagonally opposite corner. The other two corners will lose weight.
- If you lower the ride height at a given corner, that corner will lose weight as will the diagonally opposite corner. The other two corners will gain weight.
- This will not change left-side or rear weight percentages.
- To add weight to a given corner, raise the ride height at that corner, or lower the ride height at an adjacent corner. For example, if your initial setup is 52 percent crossweight, and you want 50 percent crossweight,

lowering the right-front or left-rear corner will decrease crossweight percentage. You could also raise the left-front or right-rear ride heights to do the same thing.

- It is best to make small changes at each corner, instead of a big change at one corner. This keeps the ride heights as close to ideal as possible. In the above example, to go from 52 percent to 50 percent crossweight, try lowering the right-front and left-rear one-half turn on the spring perch or by removing spring spacers, and raise the left-front and right-rear the same amount.
- Always record the crossweights and ride heights for reference at the racetrack if changes are needed.
- Measure control arm angles after each change. The angles are another way to set the suspension for the desired ride height and crossweight percentage.
- The distance from the ground to an inner suspension arm pivot point will also accomplish the above goal.
- Remember that stagger changes, tire pressure changes, and spring changes will change the ride height and alter the crossweight percentage.

Changes at the track:
- Make small changes at the track, and make only one change at a time.
- If the car understeers or oversteers in only one direction, check the crossweight percentage.

One of the most important aspects of racing is a good handling balance. Setting static weight distribution and adjusting crossweight percentage is one way to assure good handling. Taking the time and making the effort always pays dividends.

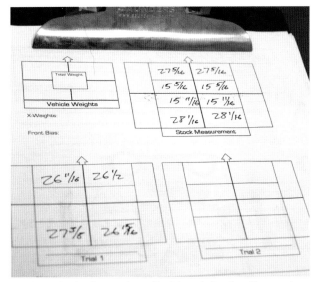

This chart makes keeping records easy. The data can be transferred to a spread sheet program for additional analysis. Always keep records of vehicle weights and percentages. *Hotchkis Sport Suspension*

Corner weights are proportional to ride heights. A quick and pretty accurate way to measure ride height at one corner is to measure from the ground to the lip of the wheel well. A small change in height can make a significant change in corner weights. *Hotchkis Sport Suspension*

Coil-over springs/shocks provide the quickest and easiest way to adjust ride heights. *Progress Technology/Jeff Cheechov*

## EASY AND SIMPLE SETUP TRICKS

Suspension setup is a crucial factor in achieving peak handling performance. But some of the tools, such as scales and laser alignment equipment, are very expensive. One solution is to get a group of racers together to share equipment; you can also borrow equipment, if that's an option. But the reality is you can get 99 percent of the work done with some basic equipment. For less than $100, you can get your car set up, and then all you really need is a tire pyrometer (as low $99) and a stop watch. Here's what you need:

- Machinist's rule
- Plumb bob
- Level
- Angle finder
- Tape measure
- Angle Iron or Plate (steel or aluminum)

### Check Toe with String

A roll of survey string, available at any hardware store, is all you need to quickly check front toe. The string must be held so that it passes around the outside of the rear tire and touches both the front and rear sidewall bulges at axle height. Roll your car back and forth on a flat, level surface so that the tires track as straight as possible. Unroll the string and, with the string taut, slowly move the string until it just touches either the front or rear sidewall bulge, again at axle height. Measure the gap with a machinist's rule at the end not touching the sidewall. The measurement is the toe-out if the gap is at the rear and toe-in if the gap is at the front. If the string does not contact both the front and rear bulge of the rear tire sidewall, either the rear axle is offset, or the rear

axle is out of alignment. Keep in mind that this method will not work on race cars where the rear track width varies more than one inch from the front track width.

### Check Front and Rear Toe with Plumb Bobs

First put a true scribe mark around the tire. Then place a one-inch-long piece of masking tape on the floor where the plumb bobs will touch. Next lay string with plumb bobs accurately over the scribe line so that the tips of the plumb bobs just clear the floor. Let the plumb bobs stabilize and carefully mark the floor where the plumb bobs come to rest. Do this on both sides and use a tape measure to measure between the marks. This is a very accurate way to measure toe if the scribe lines are accurate.

An even more accurate way to do this is to use aluminum or steel angle iron a few inches longer than the diameter of your tires. Carefully notch each end for the plumb bob string so that the notch is in exactly the same location at each end. Mount the angle iron to the brake rotor with either reversed lug nuts or clamps and level the angle iron. Mark the floor where the plumb bobs come to rest as above and repeat on the opposite side. Take measurements on the floor between the marks. You can also use this method to check rear axle housing toe.

### Square the Steering Arms

The box formed by the steering arm, idler arm, and drag link must be square to avoid unwanted bump steer. The distance between pivot points of the steering must be measured accurately. Center the steering by rolling the car forward at least one full tire revolution. With a tape, measure between the steering arm and idler arm pivots at the chassis and at the drag link. They should be identical. Adjust if needed. Then measure the diagonals. They should also be equal. If the distance between pivots is equal, but the diagonals are unequal, something is bent. Take a close look.

## Bump Steer

Bump steer is toe change during vertical wheel travel. You can use the same setup as in "Check Front and Rear Toe with Plumb Bobs" above to measure bump steer. Just disconnect the spring and shock (with the chassis on stands) and use a jack to raise and lower the suspension. Start with the suspension at ride height and mark the tape on the floor. This is your baseline. As you raise and lower the suspension, the marks will move usually inward with zero bump steer. If one end moves farther from the baseline than the other end, bump steer is present. The difference in measurements is the amount of bump steer. If the front measurement is bigger, you have toe-out, if the rear is bigger you have toe-in. Plot the change at one-inch increments for two inches of bump and two inches of rebound travel at each front wheel. Usually, changing the mounting height of the inner or outer pivot points on the tie rod will influence the amount of bump steer. You can tell which way to go by looking at the tie rod ball joints in relationship to the inner and outer pivot points of the upper, or in some cases lower, control arms. The tie rod ends should be in the exact plane as the line between the upper and lower ball joints on the outer end and the upper

and lower control arm pivots on the inner end. Raising or lowering the tie rod ends will often align the tie rod ball joints exactly with the lines between upper and lower pivot points. Spacers can often be used to do this.

## Caster

Use an angle finder on a vertical location on the front spindles. This may not be completely accurate for actual caster angle, but it allows you to get back to the initial setting after you have modified your suspension or made another change.

## Camber

Camber should really be set by tire temps, so knowing a camber angle in advance is not important. But once you get the tire temps right, you need to know the camber angle so that you can repeat the setup at the track. Make sure the car is on level ground before measuring. You can use a straight edge against the tire with an angle finder (be sure to avoid the raised letters on the sidewall) or place the angle finder on the upper control arm. Its angle is directly related to the camber angle at that wheel.

## Panhard Bar Setting

If your car has a Panhard bar on the rear suspension, use an angle finder on the Panhard bar for an angle. Most Panhard bars are not adjustable, but if yours is, try to keep it level at static ride height.

A good handling track car starts out with a good setup in the shop before leaving for the track. *Eibach Springs*

## Crossweight

While scales are the easiest way to do this, the crossweight is determined by ride heights. Change a ride height and the crossweight changes. If you do not have access to scales for a baseline, set the rear ride height to the measurement recommended by the suspension package manufacturer, and level side to side. Set the front slightly lower, but also level side to side. At the track you can tune the chassis by changing ride heights in very small amounts—½ to a full turn—while trying to keep any single corner of the chassis from getting too high or low. Keep notes and do this until the car handles the same in left and right turns. Recheck the ride heights and now you have a setup that works. It is a lot more time-consuming, but you don't need scales to get there.

Front-drive cars should have weight as equal as possible on both left and right front tires with a crossweight percentage of 50 percent. This helps maximize tire traction for acceleration. *Eibach Springs*

Drag cars need perfect crossweights and suspension alignments that minimize rolling resistance. *Eibach Springs*

### Rear Axle Alignment

For a solid rear axle suspension, a simple tape measure is all you need. Measure from a lateral frame rail forward of the axle housing to the rear axle housing. The trick is finding a spot on each side of the housing that is square. Better yet, drop a plumb bob from the hub on the axle centerline on each side and draw a line through each mark. Measure from the line to an identical spot on the left and right sides of the lateral frame rail. Now you have a very accurate measurement. The rear axle housing is out of alignment if the measurements are not identical.

### Brake Bias

Most likely, you do not have a way to adjust brake bias without installing a brake proportioning valve. But if you do, significant performance gains can be made while braking. Brake bias is best set on the track with an observer watching for wheel lock up at one end of the car first. Just use old tires.

You can get in the ballpark with a torque wrench. With the car on stands, have someone apply the brakes until one end locks up. Use the torque wrench on a wheel lug and measure the torque it takes to turn the wheel. Apply more pressure until the other end just locks up. Check the torque at the first end again. The front should lock up first, and due to weight transfer the front should require some amount of torque higher than the rear. Test the bias on the straightaway with an observer before you run at speed on the track.

### Scaling

You need to know what your car weighs and the corner weights. If you don't have scales, try to use the track scales, or borrow old grain scales. If all else fails, use local official truck scales, so that you have a place to start.

### Rear-end Trueness

It is important to know if the rear axle is straight, or has camber and/or toe. We checked toe-in "Check Front and Rear Toe with Plumb Bobs" earlier. Use the angle finder on the brake rotor for camber. Be sure the car is level on jack stands. A little toe-in is OK, up to ⅛ inch. A little negative camber is OK, up to ³⁄₁₆ inch. More of either, or any toe-out or positive camber, requires that the rear axle housing be straightened.

### Wheel and Brake Rotor Runout

Clamp a scribe or pointed punch to a weighted (for stability) jack stand. Place the end of the scribe against the wheel rim at the bead or against a brake rotor. Rotate the wheel or rotor until you find the high spot and position the scribe. Rotate the wheel or rotor until you find the low spot and use a machinist's rule to measure the gap. That is the amount of runout. Check with the wheel or rotor manufacturer about runout tolerances. Too much wheel runout will have an effect similar to bump steer, and rotor runout will cause brake pad kickback, which you can often feel in the brake pedal under hard braking. Rotor runout hurts braking performance.

Rally cars not only need lots of travel when jumps are part of the course, but if they have any bump steer at all, a one-wheel-at-a-time landing can become very hairy. *Eibach Springs*

# Chapter 8
# Suspension Tuning for the Track

Assuming you have a well-engineered and tested suspension system to begin with, the key to fast laps and good handling characteristics is suspension tuning. Tuning is a complex endeavor, requiring a great deal of focus and commitment. Successful suspension and chassis tuning requires finding the best series of compromises for each element of the suspension system. But if you always keep in mind a single, crucial fact, you will make progress much more quickly. *Never forget that the goal is to increase tire traction and balance!*

There will be times that a representative of your shock or spring manufacturer will be at the track. When you ask for his assistance to solve a handling problem, 99 times out of 100, he'll want to fix the problem with the component his company makes. While this may be useful, it is often—in fact, most often—not the best solution. You must keep in mind that the whole system, including the driver, must be considered when analyzing handling problems and searching for solutions. And the first clues you should look for are found in the tire temperatures. Tire temps and good driver feedback are key elements, short of a good data logger and an engineer to help interpret the data.

The logical place to start tuning is with the tires. Beyond tires, there is no particular order to what component needs to be considered, but always consider all of them before making changes.

The one with the most traction for the duration of the event will be fastest. *Falken Tire*

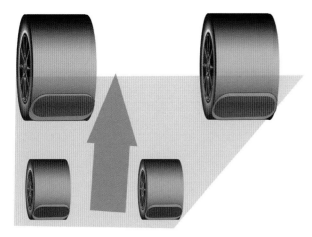

Shocks, springs, and anti-roll bars are used to manipulate weight transfer and therefore transient traction. This diagram shows weight transfer to the rear during acceleration.

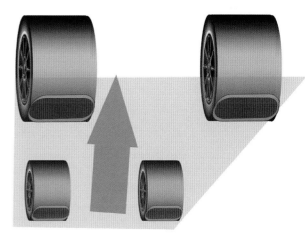

This diagram shows weight transfer to the front during deceleration.

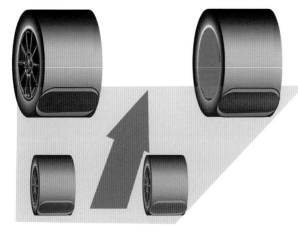

This diagram shows weight transfer to the rear and outside during acceleration while exiting a turn.

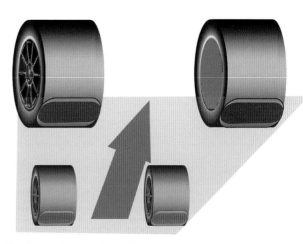

This diagram shows weight transfer to the front and outside during deceleration.

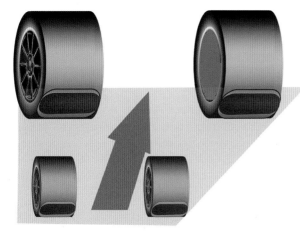

At rest or moving in a straight line with no acceleration shows equal loads on all four tire contact patches.

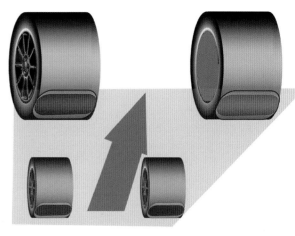

An oversteer condition will cause more heat to build in the rear tires.

## TUNING TIRES

There are several ways to alter handling balance. You can change spring rates, bar rates, crossweight, suspension geometry, shock rates, roll center location, tire pressure, or static weight distribution. But handling balance is only part of the story. The goal for any racing situation is to get maximum traction from the tires, hopefully all of the tires. Each tire is capable of making so much traction on a given car and under given track conditions. Nothing you do can cause the tires to make more traction than that limit. But how you tune the chassis and work the tire contact patches will determine how much traction you actually have available. The goal is to minimize the loss. A key way to do this is to optimize the tire's contact with the track surface and optimize the load on all four tire contact patches relative to a given spot on the racetrack, mid-turn, corner entry, or corner exit. While not a factor for street driving, any form of motorsports competition requires the optimization of tire traction at each tire contact patch and at the highest possible level of grip from all four tires. And this includes, to a slightly lesser degree, track day driving events, if for no other reason than it is not fun—and can be dangerous—to drive an ill-handling car at speed on a track.

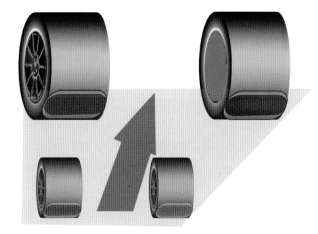

An understeer condition will cause too much heat to build in the front tires.

So how do you know what's going on? The best way is to monitor tire temperatures. Tire temperatures tell the traction tale very effectively. The good news is, tire pyrometers are inexpensive, easy to use, and the single most important tool you can own to get a car setup dialed-in. But there are some techniques you need to know to get the best possible data.

Tire temperatures tell the story along with driver input and data logging.

## TAKING TIRE TEMPERATURES

Here are some important tips for taking tire temperatures:

- Always take temperatures, even if the car is out only for one or two laps.
- Take temps after the event when possible.
- Record temps and pressures.
- Use a tire temperature chart.
- Take temps at three spots on each tire about one inch from each edge and in the middle.
- Always take temps in the same lateral spot on the tire tread.
- Always take temps in the same order on the tire—either inside or outside first, then the middle.
- Always start at the same tire.
- Always go around the car in the same direction.
- Move fast. Tires cool quickly, giving inaccurate readings if too much time elapses. The heat will also equalize across the tire. The temperature difference grows smaller as time passes.
- While moving fast is important, make sure that each reading has stabilized before moving the probe to the next spot. Removing the probe from a spot too soon can cause inaccurate readings.
- Unless you use a memory pyrometer, have one crew member record temps while the other takes the readings. If no crew member is available for recording, the driver can record the data while sitting in the car.
- The fourth tire in the sequence will lose heat by the time the temps are taken. After the fourth tire is measured, check the first tire again so that you can see the change in temps from the first readings. This will give you an idea of how hot the other tires were while the first tire was being checked. This is an important part of the procedure.
- Take tire pressures right after taking the temperatures. Go in the same order. Also record pressures just before the car goes on to the racetrack so that you can measure the pressure gain.

- Once in a while, check tire pressures after 5 to 10 minutes. If the pressure is higher than when the car entered the pits, the extra heat causing the pressure increase has come from the brakes. Tires have been known to blow out (a long time ago) sitting in the pits due to heat and pressure buildup from brake heat. If the pressures go up, you have a potential brake heat problem.
- The needle on the probe should be inserted into the tire tread. The heat in the tire tread is more stable and cools more slowly below the tread surface.
- Keep heat in the probe by holding your thumb or finger over the needle while taking the temps.
- Slide the probe over the tire tread surface when moving the probe across the tire. This keeps the probe hotter while moving it across the tire and reduces the time for the probe to get up to peak temperature.
- A higher priced pyrometer often has a more sensitive probe, reducing time to get up to temperature.
- Using more than one pyrometer can get temps faster and give more accurate readings.
- Taking tire temperatures at different locations around the track will give you different information about what the tires are doing under different conditions of braking, cornering, or accelerating. This can prove to be very helpful in solving handling problems at different points on the track.
- The driver should avoid hard braking coming into the pits (or wherever the tire temps are taken). The hard braking will put excessive heat in the front tires compared to the rear.
- The driver should not take a cool down lap. The tires will cool too quickly, giving false readings.

Taking tire temperatures is a crucial link in the chassis tuning process. Be religious about taking temps and recording the appropriate information. It will come in handy.

Taking tire temperatures should be routine even with a data logger on board. Here the crew from Progress works with the author to analyze tire temps. *Progress Technology*

# CHASSIS TUNING TRICKS USING TIRE TEMPERATURES

Your race car is perfectly balanced through the corners. It gets into the turns quickly, and corner exit is strong, but you consistently lose one or two car lengths in mid-turn. Toe is correct, roll couple seems good, crossweights seem right. What could cause the car to be slow in mid-turn? The answer is a lack of total traction.

The goal when you set up your race car is to get maximum traction as well as create a good balance all the way around the racetrack. If, for some reason, maximum traction is not there, the car will not perform to its peak at some point on, or all the way around the racetrack. One of the most important jobs a racer has is to get the maximum traction possible out of the tires. Here are a few tricks to help you accomplish that goal.

## 1. Consider All Four Tires

The goal is to get the most traction possible from all four tires. The harder each tire works, the more traction the car will have, and the faster the car can enter, get through, and exit the corners. One sign of how hard a tire is working (and therefore the tire's traction) is the average temperature of the tire. There are two types of tire temperature averages: the average for a single tire, and the average of pairs of tires (such as diagonal, side, or end). If the average temperature for a single tire is higher than the maximum temperature for your type of tires, that tire is working too hard. If the average temperature is lower than the other average temperatures of the other tires, then that tire is not doing enough work and your car will not perform as well as it could. The colder tire needs to work harder and you need to figure out how to do that.

Comparing average tire temperatures can offer a wealth of information:

- The cold tire needs to work harder.
- The hotter end of the car is losing traction before the colder end. If the rear average temp is hotter than the front, the car is oversteering; if the front average is hotter, the car is understeering. This could indicate a change in roll couple distribution (spring rates and/or sway bar rates).
- If one side (left or right) has an average tire temperature hotter than the other side, more static weight on the cooler would help.
- Diagonal average tire temps will offer clues about crossweights for a given situation.

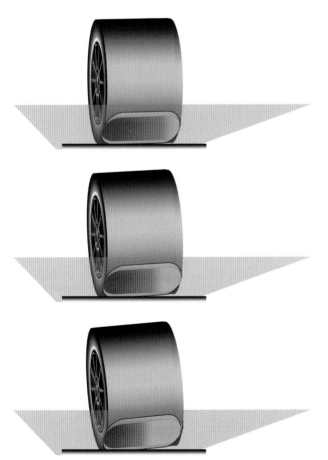

Too little camber in the tire will cause more heat towards the outside of the tire.

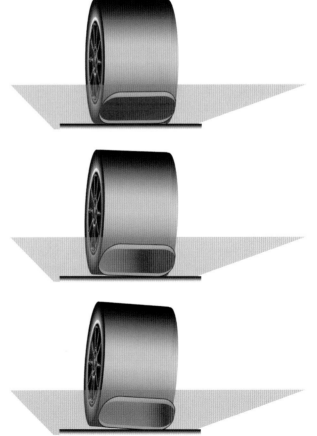

Too much camber in the tire will cause more heat towards the inside of the tire.

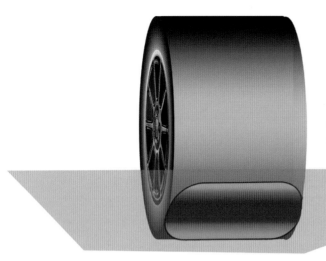

When camber is correct, load, heat, and wear are evenly distributed on the tire contact patch. A tire with this load distribution makes the most traction.

### 2. Look at the Complete Tire Contact Patch

While the average tire temperature for a given tire provides a good comparison for overall traction, the individual tire temperatures at a given tire offer solid information about what is happening at each tire contact patch. Comparing individual tire temperatures at a given tire can tell you how to tune that tire:

- If an edge of a tire is hotter, the camber is off.
- If the middle of the tire is hotter or colder, the pressure is off.

### 3. Always Take Tire Temps

Tire temps are the only link you have to what is happening at the tire contact patch. You need to know what is happening, so always take tire temps, even after a race.

### 4. When Possible, Take Tire Temps at Different Locations on the Racetrack

The habit is to take tire temps in the pits. On a test day, you may be able to take tire temps at any point on the racetrack. This can give you important information about what the tires are doing under a variety of conditions. For example, if you measure temps coming off a corner, you will see how the tires are working at this critical point on the track. Naturally, the rear tires should be hotter in this situation, just as the fronts should be hotter under hard braking. Keep these facts in mind when taking tire temps at various points.

- When you stop to take temps, slow down gently or too much heat will build in the front tires, unless you are measuring corner entry temps.
- When you analyze temps, take into account where you took the temps.

- Mid-turn setup is best when all tire temps are close to equal.
- Front temps should be hotter at corner entry, but as close to equal (left to right) as possible.
- Rears should be equal, but hotter than fronts at corner exit.

### 5. Pay Attention to Static Weight Distribution

One way to get average tire temps closer together and to increase total traction is to look at the temps and compare them to static weight distribution. If a tire is more than 15 to 20 degrees cooler, that tire needs more static weight on it. More static weight on a cold tire means more dynamic weight on the same tire while cornering, and less on another tire. This will most often improve overall traction, although handling balance may need to be re-established.

### 6. Dynamic Weight Distribution Is a Key

The goal is to have weight distribution as equal as possible at rest so that the average tire load is the same during left and right turns. This creates the optimum dynamic weight distribution out on the track. Tire temps can give us the same basic information, and allow you to make good judgments about improving setup.

### 7. Heat in the Tires Tells the Story

If the tire has heat, it's making traction, up to the point that the tire gets too hot. When all the tires are in the optimum range of operating temperature, you are getting maximum traction. Anything less than that indicates your race car could be getting around the track faster. Here are some important facts to keep in mind.

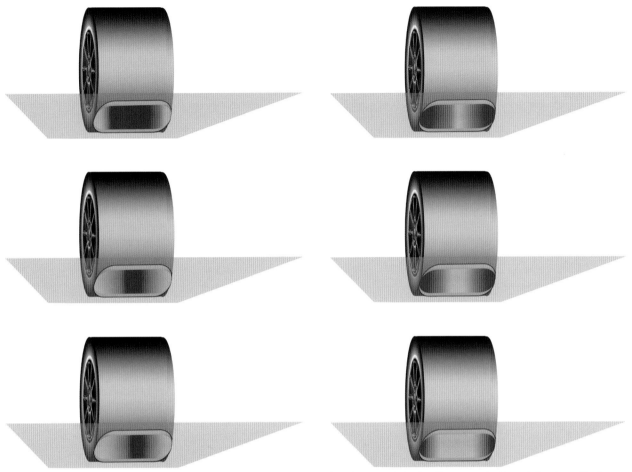

Too much pressure in the tire will cause more heat towards the middle of the tire. | Too little pressure in the tire will cause more heat towards the edges of the tire.

- If any tire is overheated, it is doing too much work. A change is needed.
- If all tires are overheated, the compound may be too soft for the car and conditions.
- If front tires are overheating, it may that the driver is using the brakes too hard while steering.
- If the rear tires are overheating, the driver may be using too much throttle exiting the corners, causing wheelspin.
- If temps are too cool overall, it could be the ambient weather conditions. If it's cold, take that into account.
- If average temps are too cold, it could be the driver. If the driver is not up to speed, temps will never get to optimum and handling problems should be nearly non-existent. The driver needs to push the car closer to the limits of traction before any setup issues can be resolved with any clarity.

## 8. Put Heat Where You Need It

If a tire is colder than the rest, figure out how to get more heat there. Here are some tips.

- Start with static weight distribution. Put weight on the cold tire without sacrificing the overall vertical load balance of the car as a whole.
- If the front or rear is colder, put more roll couple distribution (stiffer springs/bars) at the colder end.
- If the diagonal average temperatures are off, check crossweights.
- Toe and bump steer can be used to get heat on the inside of the front tires.

What happens at the tire contact patch is all we really care about when trying to get the maximum traction from a race car. Nothing else really matters. Tire temperatures are the easiest and most cost-effective link you have to the action at the tire contact patch. Using the tire temperatures effectively can pay considerable dividends on the racetrack. It's worth the effort.

With the right suspension components, adjusting camber is quick. *Progress Technology*

# CHASSIS TUNING WITH AVERAGE TIRE TEMPERATURES

At your home track, you're fast, but cannot maintain quite as much cornering speed as your closest competitor. You go through mid-turn and the exit of the turns just a little bit faster. You've been monitoring tire temperatures all season, and the temps look good. All of the inside temps are just a little hotter than the outside, and the middle temps are right in between. Pressures and camber are dialed. What else can you do?

You know that tire temperatures offer clues about traction at each tire contact patch, but what about comparing one tire, or pair of tires, to the others? The average tire temps are another clue you can use to find more traction.

Average tire temperatures are found for each tire by adding the three temp readings together then dividing by 3. In addition to the average temperature at each tire, you will want to know the average temperatures for the left side and right side, the front and the rear, and the two diagonals. The goal is to get the average temps of each tire as close as possible to each other. This means that each tire is doing as much work as possible. If one tire is much hotter, or cooler, then tuning may make your car faster. It is important to have a basic understanding of tuning the chassis, especially with tire temperatures.

Average tire temperature clues can tell the effectiveness of static weight distribution, how crossweight is affecting the car, if the roll couple distribution is in the ball park, brake balance, how the driver is using the controls, and if there may be chassis alignment problems.

Always look at the individual temps because they will still tell you how well that tire contact patch is working on the track surface. Use the individual temps to tune pressures first, then camber.

Here some examples of tire temps and their interpretation:

### Tire Temperature Analysis

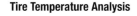
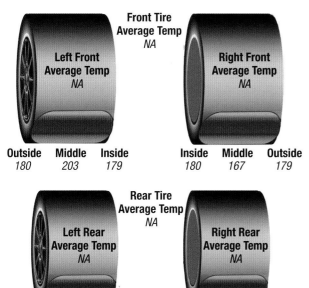

| Left Front Average Temp NA | | | Right Front Average Temp NA | | |
|---|---|---|---|---|---|
| Outside | Middle | Inside | Inside | Middle | Outside |
| 180 | 203 | 179 | 180 | 167 | 179 |

Front Tire Average Temp NA

| Left Rear Average Temp NA | | | Right Rear Average Temp NA | | |
|---|---|---|---|---|---|
| Outside | Middle | Inside | Inside | Middle | Outside |
| 184 | 173 | 186 | 175 | 198 | 174 |

Rear Tire Average Temp NA

Left Tire Average Temp    NA     Right Tire Average Temp    NA

Right Front/Left Rear Average Temp    NA     Right Rear/Left Front Average Temp    NA

**Tire Temperature Chart 1**
This chart shows pressures that are not correct. The RIGHT FRONT pressure is too low, the LEFT FRONT is too high, the LEFT REAR is too low and the RIGHT REAR is too high. It takes practice to determine how much to change the pressure for a given set of conditions. The greater the difference, the greater the change needs to be to get the contact patch flat on the racetrack. Keep in mind that when the center temp is hotter, the pressure is too high, and if the center temp is cooler, the pressure is too low. *Note: Average tire temperatures are meaningless when tire pressures are not optimized.*

### Tire Temperature Analysis

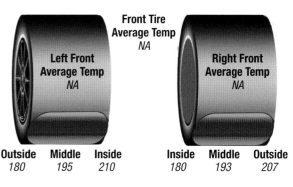
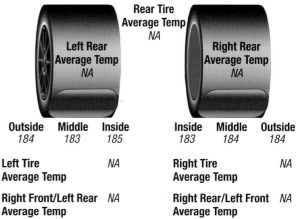

| Left Front Average Temp NA | | | Right Front Average Temp NA | | |
|---|---|---|---|---|---|
| Outside | Middle | Inside | Inside | Middle | Outside |
| 180 | 195 | 210 | 180 | 193 | 207 |

Front Tire Average Temp NA

| Left Rear Average Temp NA | | | Right Rear Average Temp NA | | |
|---|---|---|---|---|---|
| Outside | Middle | Inside | Inside | Middle | Outside |
| 184 | 183 | 185 | 183 | 184 | 184 |

Rear Tire Average Temp NA

Left Tire Average Temp    NA     Right Tire Average Temp    NA

Right Front/Left Rear Average Temp    NA     Right Rear/Left Front Average Temp    NA

**Tire Temperature Chart 2**
The front camber is off in this chart. At the left-front, the wheel needs less negative camber to heat the outside edge of the tire. The right-front needs more negative camber. Since tires make the most traction in a corner with a small amount of dynamic negative camber, the inside edges of the front tires should show temps between 5 and 10 degrees hotter than the outside edges. This indicates that maximum traction is happening. *Note: Average tire temperatures are meaningless when tire camber angles are not optimized.*

## INFRARED TIRE PYROMETERS

One of latest innovations in setup equipment is the infrared pyrometer. Their biggest advantage is speed. The biggest drawback is consistency. Infrared averages heat over the area within the field of view of its lens. The area the lens reads is proportional to the distance the lens is held from the heat source. Since we need to monitor as little as one degree of temperature differential from one spot to the next on a tire, if too large an area is read, or if the area is inconsistent in size, then the data is less useful. It is very important to hold an infrared pyrometer at the exact same distance from the tread surface every time the pyrometer is used. And it needs to be held close enough to the tread so that a spot only about one inch wide is monitored. An advantage to this type of pyrometer is that by holding the lens at the proper distance, you can get an average tire temperature for each tire very easily; but again, the distance must be accurate and consistent. Finally, even though the infrared pyrometer reads temps very quickly, it reads the surface temp only, and the surface cools and temperature balances more quickly than the rubber below the surface. Keep these facts in mind, and good results can be achieved with an infrared pyrometer.

## CHASSIS TUNING WITH SPRINGS

At the last event, your car was very quick. During registration for this event, one of your fellow drivers asks about what springs you run. You tell him. He changes his springs to what you run. In practice, his car understeers right off the track. The understeer was extreme and your fellow driver, unhurt but embarrassed and mad, thinks you lied to him about your spring rates. You didn't. He just has a different model of car than you and the wheel rates and suspension frequencies are different on his car, so the information he got from you was not only useless, but when used, caused him to go off the track

This is only one of the pitfalls when tuning the chassis with springs. Tuning handling balance (push vs. loose) with springs is a common practice in racing, and rightfully so. Springs exercise a large influence on handling balance. But handling balance is not the only job the springs must accomplish. In fact, it is not even the most important job.

### Tire Temperature Analysis

**Front Tire Average Temp** 183

**Left Front Average Temp** 192

| Outside | Middle | Inside |
|---|---|---|
| 190 | 192 | 193 |

**Right Front Average Temp** 176

| Inside | Middle | Outside |
|---|---|---|
| 178 | 177 | 175 |

**Rear Tire Average Temp** 183

**Left Rear Average Temp** 177

| Outside | Middle | Inside |
|---|---|---|
| 174 | 177 | 181 |

**Right Rear Average Temp** 189

| Inside | Middle | Outside |
|---|---|---|
| 183 | 189 | 194 |

**Left Tire Average Temp** 185

**Right Tire Average Temp** 182

**Right Front/Left Rear Average Temp** 177

**Right Rear/Left Front Average Temp** 191

**Tire Temperature Chart 3**

The left-rear is in the ball park with the inside a little hotter than the outside. The right-rear is the opposite, which is undesirable. The rear axle, if solid, could be bent or out of alignment. With independent rear suspension, the right needs more negative camber. Both fronts could use more negative camber and the right front could use a little more load by increasing crossweight percentage (raising right-front and/or left-rear ride heights slightly or lowering the diagonally opposite ride heights slightly). But be careful. These temps were taken in the pit area after a run, and the last turn was a left-hander, so the left side temps are both a little lower than the right side and the left turn is the likely reason.

### Tire Temperature Analysis

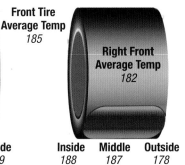

**Front Tire Average Temp** 185

**Left Front Average Temp** 189

| Outside | Middle | Inside |
|---|---|---|
| 185 | 191 | 199 |

**Right Front Average Temp** 182

| Inside | Middle | Outside |
|---|---|---|
| 188 | 187 | 178 |

**Rear Tire Average Temp** 180

**Left Rear Average Temp** 177

| Outside | Middle | Inside |
|---|---|---|
| 174 | 177 | 181 |

**Right Rear Average Temp** 183

| Inside | Middle | Outside |
|---|---|---|
| 183 | 183 | 182 |

**Left Tire Average Temp** 183

**Right Tire Average Temp** 182

**Right Front/Left Rear Average Temp** 181

**Right Rear/Left Front Average Temp** 186

**Tire Temperature Chart 4**

Look at the front tire temps, which are nearly perfect at first glance. This temperature pattern can be caused by too much toe-out at the front. The camber, which looks good here, could be off, costing tire traction, but the excessive toe-out masks the real problem. For this reason, it is important to routinely check toe. A slight bump or wear can change toe settings and hide other problems.

The primary job of the springs in a track application is to keep the tire contact patch loaded and on the racing surface over bumps and ruts. If a spring is too soft, it will oscillate or bounce, causing an uneven vertical load on the tire. If a spring is too stiff, the tire will unload too much over bumps, even losing contact with racing surface. As you know, reducing load on a tire reduces traction, so the spring has a very important job.

The secondary job of the spring is to help control the oversteer/understeer (loose/push) handling balance of the chassis. The springs work with anti-roll bars (sway bars) to do this as well as control the degree of body roll while cornering. The springs and bars work together to control where transferred weight goes, front vs. rear. The amount of weight transferred at the front vs. the rear changes vertical loading on the tires, which changes traction. When the front springs (or anti-roll bar) are stiffened, while the rears remain the same,

more weight transfer occurs at the front. This increases the load on the outside front tire, which increases traction. The traction change is slower than the increase in load at the front; and at the rear, the traction loss is slower than the decrease in load. The front also has more weight to carry, so it must work harder to corner the extra weight, and the rear will work less hard. The outcome is that with the front stiffness increased vs. the rear, the front has relatively less traction while the rear has more, so the car will tend towards the understeer direction of handling balance.

The relationship between the front spring and anti-roll bar rates and those at the rear is called roll couple distribution. It is called roll couple because it is actually the resistance to roll that manipulates which end of the car more weight will be transferred to. The springs and anti-roll bars create roll resistance. Increasing the spring or bar rate increases roll resistance and that causes a larger percentage of the weight being transferred to go to the end with the increased roll resistance.

The amount of roll resistance provided by a given set of springs and anti-roll bar can be calculated for each end of a car. Then the total roll resistance for the car is found by adding the roll resistance from both ends. The roll couple distribution can be expressed as a percentage of the front roll resistance compared to the total resistance for the whole vehicle. The front roll resistance is simply divided by total roll resistance. The answer is the roll couple distribution.

Bump control is always the highest spring priority. The range of spring rates that will control the tire contact patch over bumps is fairly large. Within that range of spring rates, you can use the springs to fine tune handling balance. Changes in spring rate as small as 2 percent will affect roll couple enough to make a difference. If a larger change is necessary to achieve the desired handling balance, the anti-roll bar should be used.

## WHEEL RATES

In the scenario opening this section, one driver wanted to know the spring rates of someone's fast car. Knowing the spring rates on another car is, frankly, useless information unless it comes from your suspension manufacturer. On the other hand, knowing the wheel rates can be very useful data, up to a point.

The wheel rate of a spring is the actual rate of the spring acting at the center of the tire contact patch. The wheel rate is nothing more than the spring rate multiplied by leverage factors. Unless a spring is mounted at the centerline of the wheel, or you have an open wheel car with bellcranks and push rod suspension linkages, the wheel rate of a spring is always less than the actual spring rate.

To determine the wheel rate of a spring, we must first know the motion ratio of the suspension linkage to which the spring mounts and which moves the spring during suspension travel. Most cars have the spring mounted to the chassis at the top and to either the rear axle housing or the lower control arm

**Tire Temperature Analysis**

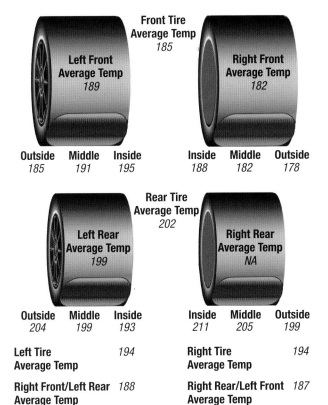

| | Front Tire Average Temp 185 | |
|---|---|---|
| **Left Front Average Temp 189** | | **Right Front Average Temp 182** |
| Outside 185 | Middle 191 | Inside 195 |
| Inside 188 | Middle 182 | Outside 178 |

| | Rear Tire Average Temp 202 | |
|---|---|---|
| **Left Rear Average Temp 199** | | **Right Rear Average Temp NA** |
| Outside 204 | Middle 199 | Inside 193 |
| Inside 211 | Middle 205 | Outside 199 |

| | | |
|---|---|---|
| **Left Tire Average Temp** | 194 | |
| **Right Tire Average Temp** | 194 | |
| **Right Front/Left Rear Average Temp** | 188 | |
| **Right Rear/Left Front Average Temp** | 187 | |

**Tire Temperature Chart 5**
Roll steer, or rear axle steer, can cause temperature patterns like those shown here. This causes scrub and heats the leading edge of the tire contact patch. Even though the average temperatures show that the car should be oversteering, this car probably understeers in left turns and oversteer in right turns. Checking rear axle alignment and crossweights will tell you how to cure the situation. The most important thing is to not be fooled by the data. You need to know what the rear suspension is doing so you can make better judgments about the setup.

at the front. Let's use the lower control arm for an example. Let's take a lower control arm that measures 16 inches from the center of the inner pivot to the center of the outer ball joint. If the spring is mounted to the lower control arm so that the exact centerline of the spring is 8.0 inches from the inner pivot center, then we can find the motion ratio by dividing the length of the control arm (16 inches) by the distance that the spring centerline is from the inner pivot center (8.0 inches). In our example, the motion ratio is 0.50.

The motion ratio actually affects the spring rate in two ways. First is the effect of leverage, like a teeter totter or pry bar. In our example, the leverage on the spring is exactly one-half, so now our spring rate is effectively 50 percent of what it would be if it were at the centerline of the wheel. But there is also the issue of travel, since we calculate springs in pounds per inch. When the wheel moves up (or down) by one inch, the spring will travel less. In our example, since the spring is 50 percent of the distance from the inner pivot to the ball joint center, then the spring will travel only 50 percent as much as the wheel. So the wheel rate of the spring is further reduced since it travels only half the distance of the wheel. In our example, if we started with a 1,000 pound per inch spring rate, the rate of that spring acting at the wheel would be 1,000 pounds times 0.50 (the leverage factor portion of the motion ratio). That result would then be multiplied by 0.50 (the travel factor of the motion ratio). Then the wheel rate of our 1,000-pound spring equals 1,000 times 0.50 times 0.50, or 1,000 times 0.50 squared. This becomes 1,000 times 0.25, which equals the

wheel rate of the spring acting at the center of the tire contact patch. This means the spring acting at the center of the tire has a rate of only 250 pounds per inch of travel.

There are two more factors that affect the wheel rate, though they are minor in most cases. The first is the mounting angle of the spring from vertical. The correction factor for the mounting angle of the spring is the cosine of the angle times the spring rate or the wheel rate. In our example, we already have a wheel rate from the motion ratio, so the solution is found by multiplying the cosine of the angle times 250. Let's say the angle is 7 degrees, not very large. The cosine of 7 degrees is .993, so the new, improved wheel rate is 250 times 0.993, or 248 pounds. This is nearly insignificant in the big picture. Angles of 10 degrees or less have very small effects on the wheel rate and can be ignored. Over 10 degrees and the effect becomes significant. At 30 degrees, for example, the cosine is .867, so the wheel rate takes a bigger hit, dropping from 250 pounds to 216 pounds.

The final factor is another motion ratio, this time from the outer ball joint of the lower control arm to the instant center of the suspension. For most cars, the arm length from the ball joint to instant center is several feet. This motion ratio is found by dividing the length of the spring centerline to instant center distance by the ball joint to instant center distance (the length of the virtual swing arm). This is usually a very large number, very close to one, so the effect is very small, unless of course the virtual swing arm is short. Keep in mind that the instant center changes length as well as moving vertically during body roll, so this effect can change as body roll changes, which means that the wheel rate can change during body roll as well. For a long virtual swing arm, say 5 feet, using our prior example, the virtual swing arm is 60 inches. The distance of the spring center to the instant center is 52 inches, so the correction factor is 0.86, which further reduces the wheel rate from 250 pounds to 216 pounds, a significant number. Since it is difficult to measure this, and more difficult to change, this factor can be ignored in most cases. If, however, you have a situation where the handling abruptly changes in mid-turn and you have ruled out any type of bind, it could be extreme lateral instant center movement during body roll. If the instant center moves inward by 48 inches at the maximum of body roll, then the front spring will effectively become softer, causing a possible loose condition as body roll increases. With the instant center now at 12 inches from the ball joint, and the center of the spring only four inches from the instant center, the correction factor is 0.33, so that wheel rate that was 216 pounds is now only 83 pounds. Big change and potential big problem as well! This can be the core of handling problems that are very difficult to figure out. A change in suspension geometry is the real cure and how to do that is well beyond the scope of this book.

Now, what about solid axles? They are a little more complex. Over two-wheel bumps, both springs are compressed equally, so the motion ration is one. The spring rate equals

Tune with springs to control the tire contact patches over bumps and to keep the chassis ride height as low as possible. *Progress Technology*

the wheel rate. Over one-wheel bumps, both springs move some. The wheel hitting the bump moves the most while the other wheel moves some, but both springs compress and influence tire contact patch control over bumps. If each spring is mounted the same distance from the tire centerline, and the spring rates are the same, then the motion ratio is still one, but only acting on the springs encountering the bump. The reason for this is the fact that the pivot point for the axle is the tire not hitting the bump. Both springs compress and the total movement is always equal to the vertical travel of the tire hitting the bump.

Here's an example. Let's say the track width is 60 inches and the springs are separated by 30 inches, each being 15 inches inboard of the tire centerline. If the tire hitting the bump travels up one inch, and the other tire does not move vertically, the spring closest to the bump will move .75 inches and the other spring will move .25 inches. The total movement is 1.0 inches. With equal spring rates, the effective wheel rate is the rate of one spring. But if the springs are different, or the mounting points left to right are not equidistant from the tire centerline, this will be different, although the trend is the same. If nothing else, symmetrical cars are easier to figure out.

The wheel rate is very important. Naturally, it is best if the wheel rate is closer to the actual spring rate. This mostly reduces the size of the spring needed to achieve a given wheel rate. For this reason, coil-over springs work better. Because the springs are smaller in diameter, the spring centerline can be mounted closer to the ball joint center, so the motion ratio is higher and smaller, lighter springs can be used to achieve the same wheel rate.

## SUSPENSION FREQUENCIES

Now that we have determined how motion ratios affect wheel rates, and that springs can be used for tuning handling balance within a narrow range of spring rates, let's look at the best, most scientific method of determining how stiff a spring should be for the bumpiness of a track. The general rule of thumb is that the bumpier the track surface the softer the spring rate. But how soft is too soft, or not soft enough? Certainly testing, driver input, observation, and lap times are good ways to determine this, but these take time, money, and experience. The easiest way, once you have overcome that math phobia, is to use suspension frequencies.

A frequency, as the word implies, is how often an event occurs. For an object that oscillates or bounces, like a spring, we measure the frequency in cycles per second, or CPS. One cycle per second for a spring means that the springs will compress fully, extend beyond normal free height, and compress back to static loaded height once per second. One CPS is actually the low end of the range of frequencies for a suspension spring, with 3 CPS being towards the high end.

Any time a suspension spring encounters a disturbance in the road surface, the spring will compress or extend. It will continue to oscillate at its natural frequency until friction reduces or stops the movement or another disturbance disrupts the motion. On vehicles, we use shock absorbers to control and stop these oscillations. The frequency that the spring will naturally bounce at is closely related to the severity of the bumps it encounters. Very small bumps have small amplitudes or vertical displacement of the suspension. In fact, if we encountered no bumps at all we could have a rigid suspension (or no suspension) and an infinitely high suspension frequency.

Going to the other extreme, on a very bumpy road, the amplitudes, or vertical wheel movements, are very big. We need very low frequencies to allow the tire contact patch to stay in touch with the road or track surface. Higher frequencies will cause the tire to skate, even bounce over the surface, and a tire with little or no vertical load doesn't provide much in the way of traction, let alone confidence-inspiring performance. You probably wouldn't notice, though, since at high suspension frequencies over serious bumps, your eyes would be vibrating so much you couldn't see a thing. It should be obvious that when the tire contact patch is skating over bumps that the springs are too stiff. But how do you know the proper spring rate to install?

Suspension frequencies range from the ultra smooth asphalt speedway with a frequency of 3.2 CPS down to the very bumpy road or track at 1.2 CPS. Most tracks are in the middle, and the optimum suspension frequency for a track day car, autocrosser, or time attack car on a moderately bumpy road course or parking lot will be about 1.9 to 2.2 CPS.

These frequencies are for the stiffer end of the car. The front should be a different frequency than the rear. If they are the same, at a given road speed over certain types of bumps, the like frequencies will cause an oscillation between the front and rear, creating a bucking motion that is neither comfortable nor conducive to good traction or handling balance. You may have experienced this with a stiffly sprung tow vehicle on an interstate.

The separation between front and rear suspension frequencies should be about 10 percent. What seems to work best is for the higher frequency to be at the drive wheels. This allows the car to run with either a smaller anti-roll bar, or none at all on the drive wheel end of the vehicle. Since anti-roll bars try to lift the inside tire off of the ground in a corner, a stiffer bar can hurt traction exiting corners. The stiffer springs at the drive end help control body roll more without resorting to a stiffer bar.

There are two primary factors affecting the spring frequency. First is the weight resting on the spring, or the sprung weight. (The sprung weight is the corner weight less the weight of items not suspended by the spring, like wheels, tires, brakes, hubs and half the weight of the shocks and springs.) The frequency goes down as the sprung weight goes up for a given wheel rate. The second factor is the wheel rate. If you increase the wheel rate, the frequency gets higher.

Here is more fodder for thought. At what point on the racetrack do you want to measure the sprung weight at each corner of the car? In other words, where do you want your car to be at its optimum handling? In the shop on wheel scales, which is where most of us measure the weight? On the straights where acceleration is paramount? How about in the turns?

The only place we can easily measure sprung weight, at least without expensive load sensors and data acquisition, is in the garage. So that's where to start. But let's make a few assumptions. If we are attempting to get the vertical load equal on all four tire contact patches during steady state cornering, then maybe we should have wheel rates that allow for equal frequencies during cornering. This would clearly give the best control over bumps in mid-turn.

The bottom line is that you must find the best compromise possible for your car, track conditions, and driving style. Tuning with springs and using suspension frequencies as a tool will help you find the best compromise possible. Knowledge and experimentation often lead to the unfair advantage. Let good judgment, common sense and lap times be the final factors in determining the best setup for your circumstances.

## TUNING WITH SHOCKS

In the middle of an event, you are running just behind the leader. He is pulling away slightly, and the place on the racetrack where he seems to gain is going into the corners under braking. You're driving in just as deep as you can, but the leader is able to drive in half a car length deeper. If you go in that hard you pick up a push. The car is great everywhere else, and you can run with the leader. Your cars are identical

and on the same tires, so where could his advantage be? It's a frustrating race, even though you finish second, because you just can't quite run with the leader.

This scenario could be improved by making a shock change. The trick is defining the problem, determining where it happens, and making the best choice to help cure the problem. A key word here is PROBLEM. Shocks really don't cure problems, but they can be great for making small improvements in handling in specific parts of the track or in a corner. Shocks can be used to fine-tune the handling balance of a car during transitions. Shocks will not cure a big handling problem, though they can cause handling problems if they are bent, bind, or way too stiff or soft.

First, shocks affect how fast weight is transferred. Second, this changes the tire loading while the shock is still moving in either bump or rebound travel.

## HOW SHOCKS AFFECT HANDLING

The shock controls how fast weight is transferred. This affects the load on a tire and can change the handling balance while weight is being transferred. Once all weight has been transferred, the shock no longer influences handling. Since weight is almost always being transferred, the shocks are almost always affecting handling balance.

In general, rebound damping controls how quickly weight leaves a tire while bump controls how quickly weight goes onto a tire. Stiffer valving causes a shock to react more quickly; softer valving slows the reaction of the shock. Stiffer valving gets the load to change more quickly. Stiffer rebound valving gets the load off a tire more quickly and onto the diagonally opposite tire faster going in to or out of a corner. Stiffer bump valving gets the load onto that tire faster. If all the valving—both bump

At this moment the blue Dodge needs as much weight going onto the rear tires as possible for acceleration off the turn. This can be done with stiffer front rebound and stiffer rear bump valving in the shocks. *Hotchkis Sport Suspension*

SUSPENSION TUNING FOR THE TRACK

For braking, we want to get the weight onto the front tires from the rear quickly. *Hotchkis Sport Suspension*

and rebound—at all four corners is changed equally, the effect on handling balance is minimal. If only bump or rebound is changed, then there is an effect. If only one end or one corner is changed, there is also an effect.

In road racing or autocrossing, when going into a corner, as long as the driver is moving (as opposed to holding stationary) either the steering wheel or the brake pedal, the shock has an influence on tire loading. Braking causes weight to transfer forward, compressing the front suspension and shocks, extending the rear suspension and shocks. When cornering, the weight transfers from the inside to the outside, extending the inside suspension and shocks while compressing the outside suspension and shocks. When both braking and cornering take place, as they nearly always do going into a turn, both effects occur. In a left turn, the right-front, which is compressing both from roll and pitch, and the left rear, which is extending from both factors, are moving the most and will have the biggest influence. The left-front and right-rear are receiving opposite movement from roll and pitch, reducing their movement and therefore their influence.

Mid corner, where the longitudinal forces (braking and acceleration) are small, and lateral forces (cornering) are highest, all of the shocks have an influence, but shock travel is very small and this reduces the influence.

At the exit, we basically undo what happened going into a corner. During acceleration, the rear shocks go into compression and the fronts into rebound. As cornering is reduced, the inside shocks go into compression and the outside shocks into rebound. Again using a left turn as an example, both forces occur in the exit phase of the corner,

the left-rear and right-front move the most since those shocks have forces working in the same direction while the left-front and right-rear have opposing forces. Do not take this to mean that the left-front and right-rear shocks do not influence handling in a left turn. THEY DO. The effect is just a little less. And everything reverses in a right-hand turn, so all four shocks have a big influence.

If you are drag racing, with a front driver, you want to keep weight on the front tires as long as possible. On a rear driver, you want weight to transfer to the rear as quickly as possible. If the alignment, static weight distribution and spring/bar rates are optimized, then shocks can be used to improve starting line launch acceleration. On the front driver, stiffer front rebound will hold the weight on the front a little and softer rear bump will delay weight transfer slightly. On a rear drive car, stiffer rear bump and stiffer front rebound will get weight to the rear more quickly. While not a major factor, it can be worth a tenth or so on the launch.

Let's go back to the earlier example. A slight push going into the corners keeps the driver from braking as late as the other car. Keep in mind, this is a very slight push. The car has a very good basic setup and is very fast. The car ahead is about 1/10 of second a lap faster. Shocks can be very helpful in this situation.

Under hard braking and some cornering in a left turn, the right-front is the heaviest loaded tire on most cars. A push means the front tires are exceeding optimum traction limits. We need a little more traction on the front, and little less on the rear. A big change could make the car loose going into the turns. Or changing the springs or anti-roll bar could cause a change in the perfect balance of the car on the exit. Even a shock change could do that.

For corner turn-in, we want to get the weight onto the front tires quickly. Stiffer front bump and stiffer rear rebound valving on the shocks helps. *Hotchkis Sport Suspension*

Here is a case where going to the left-rear or right-front would have an effect. Stiffer rebound on the left-rear or left-front, or softer bump on the right-front will get weight off the rear and onto the right-front more quickly. The left-front is the least useful change, since that will take the load of the left-front more quickly, slightly reducing traction there. The right-front is good change, but the best is the left-rear rebound. The left-rear in many, if not most cases has more travel in this situation than any other shock, so it is a good change to make, since it is likely to be most effective. Of course, you'll be turning right at some point, so the right-rear shock in rebound will affect right turns the most. You may or may NOT end up with the same rebound valving on the left- vs. right-rear shock.

Back to the left turn example. A stiffer shock in rebound on the left-rear will help the entry push problem. Let's say we go one click or number stiffer in both bump and rebound. We want the stiffer rebound, but what will the stiffer bump valving on the left-rear do to the handling? The stiffer bump on the left-rear could cause the car to loosen up at the exit. If it helps going in, it will likely loosen the car on the exit. Since the exit is more important than the entry for faster lap times, this may not be such a good change.

In most cases where the car is really good except for one spot in a corner, the best change is using an adjustable shock, with which at least rebound settings can be changed, or use a split valve shock. You could also have a shock manufacturer custom valve a shock for you. In our example, going up one click or one valving number increases the rebound valving while the bump valving remains the same. This cures the entry push without changing the balance in mid-turn or on the exit. This is a

Once weight transfer is completed, the shocks have little effect on handling and weight transfer. *Hotchkis Sport Suspension*

Transitions from left to right turns (or vice versa) are greatly influenced by shock valving, Too soft and the car wallows; too stiff and it overreacts. *Hotchkis Sport Suspension*

really good thing. But if the push were bigger, this change may help a little, but would not cure the problem. Look somewhere else in this case.

Let's look at one more example. In this case, the car is loose on the exit. Again a shock change will only help if the car is really close to begin with. And here, the problem could be caused by the driver spinning the rear tires under acceleration. This is especially likely on a slow corner. A shock change will help a little here, but will not cure the problem. In a left turn, we could decrease the left-rear bump or decrease the right-front rebound. Decreasing the right-front rebound lets the weight get off that corner faster which would help the most, but the left-rear bump reduction would be nearly as good. Again, adjustable shocks or split valve shocks will help here.

## TUNING FOR BUMPS

A really bumpy track may require softer shocks overall, especially in bump, or compression. If one bump is upsetting the balance of the car in one or two places on the track, a change would help there but may hurt everywhere else. Here you must make a compromise.

## BASELINE SHOCKS

In 95 percent of all cases, the baseline shocks should be the ones recommended by your shock manufacturer for the type of car and track you're running. Extremely bumpy tracks may require a change to softer shocks if the car skates over the bumps or feels unstable. Many racers make the mistake of going too far away from the baseline setup and end up with an unworkable setup on the car.

This Challenger has very little chassis squat during corner exit acceleration. This is a function of suspension geometry and is not easily tunable without custom brackets being used. *Hotchkis Sport Suspension*

A straight-line slalom is a great way to test transitions and tune shock valving. The driver really needs to be on top of his game since a 600-foot slalom takes about six seconds, so tenths of seconds count. *Hotchkis Sport Suspension*

## WHEN TO TUNE WITH SHOCKS

Here are some important criteria to consider when tuning with shocks to make your car faster:

• Each tire contact patch MUST be optimized. Camber, caster, tire pressure, and toe must be right before tuning with shocks. If these aren't right you're chasing your tail and wasting time.
• Static weights and crossweight percentages must be very close to optimum.
• Make sure that there are absolutely no binds in the suspension.
• Define where the problem occurs. Often a corner exit problem is a corner entry problem not recognized by the driver. A driver can easily overcompensate for corner entry understeer, causing an oversteer condition on the exit.
• The handling problem must be small. The car should already be fast. Don't expect more than .2 to .4 second improvement in lap times.
• It takes a skilled driver who is consistent and sensitive to changes to really tune with shocks. New drivers should spend a test day making shock changes to the car to see what they do. This experience is extremely important to wring the last little bit of performance out of the car.
• Make small changes. Going up two numbers or two clicks on adjustable shocks is a big change. And only change one corner or one end of the car at a time when tuning with shocks.

Shocks are clearly a very valuable tuning tool on a track car. Understanding what a shock can do is important. Getting the desired results takes effort and skill. Don't expect too much, get a good basic setup on your car, then small shock changes can pay big dividends.

## TUNING HANDLING BALANCE WITH ANTI-ROLL BARS

Your car is perfectly balanced in left turns, but in right turns, the car turns in well, but just after turn-in, the car is loose for an instant, then the handling balance is pretty good. What's happening?

In this instance, one of the anti-roll bars is preloaded; in this case, the front bar is preloaded on the left side, and the preload is caused by the bar end link being too long. The bar stays preloaded in left turns; but in right turns, as the bar untwists, it reaches the neutral position just after turn-in, providing no roll resistance for an instant. In that instant, the car oversteers until the bar again becomes loaded.

Before hitting the track, make sure that the bar is not preloaded. Preload is adjusted with the bar's end links, which should be adjustable on a well-engineered kit. Check for preload (with the car as it will be on the track, including driver weight) by disconnecting one end link. You can easily tell if the bar has a load on it. Reattach the end link so that no load is on the bar.

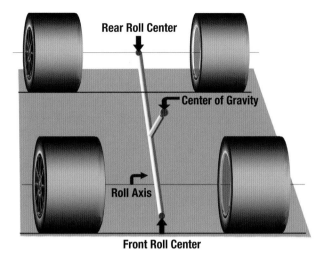

This illustration shows the relationship between the roll centers, roll axis, and center of gravity.

## TUNING ROLL COUPLE

Anti-roll bars are the best and easiest way to tune handling balance, at least if the bars are adjustable. For a track car, at least the rear bar should be adjustable. By shortening the effective length of the bar's lever arm, either by moving the slider away from the bar's end, or by moving the mounting bolt on the arm to a hole away from the bar end, you stiffen the bar. Moving in the opposite direction, closer to the bar end, will soften the bar rate.

If the anti-roll bar is too stiff at the drive wheel end of the car, there is a good chance, at least in slow corners, that the inside drive will be lifted from the surface, or at least severely unloaded, causing wheelspin as power is applied by the driver. If this occurs in more than one or two corners, then a softer anti-roll bar is called for. The bar at the opposite end will also need to be softened to maintain handling balance.

Using the bars to maximize handling balance is simple. If the car is oversteering, you can soften the rear bar, or stiffen the front bar. If both bars are adjustable, it is best to use the bar at the opposite end from the drive wheels. This reduces the lifting of the inside drive wheel off the track surface. Treat an all-wheel drive car as if it's a front drive car when tuning with the bars. If only one bar is adjustable, use that bar. If the car is understeering, then either soften the front bar or stiffen the rear bar.

## TUNING HANDLING BALANCE WITH CROSSWEIGHT

Remember that crossweight percentage affects handling balance.
Changes at the track:

• If the car understeers or oversteers in only one direction, check the crossweight percentage.
• Make small changes at the track, and make only one change at a time.

## Front Roll Center Movement
## with 5 degrees of body roll

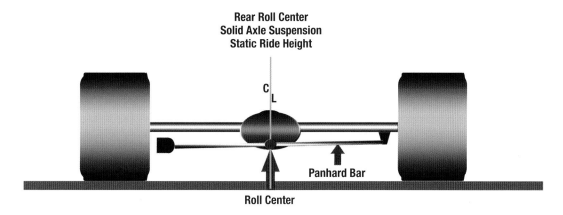

**New Roll Center**

**Original Roll Center**

This illustration shows how the roll centers can move vertically and horizontally during body roll. This is extreme, but it can happen, especially on front strut suspensions. It causes handling problems and makes it difficult for the driver to feel the car reaching the limits of traction because the suspension never settles completely.

## Rear Roll Center
## Solid Axle Suspension
## Static Ride Height

C
L

**Panhard Bar**

**Roll Center**

Here is a rear roll center diagram of a solid axle rear suspension with a lateral locating link or panhard bar.

## Front Roll Center
## Independent Suspension
## Static Ride Height

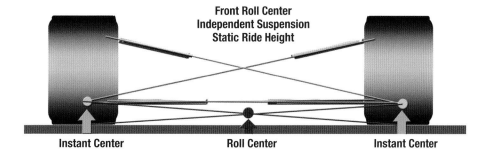

**Instant Center**

**Roll Center**

**Instant Center**

This front roll center illustration shows how the upper and lower control arms are extended to pinpoint the instant center and then the roll center. The roll center is dependent upon the geometry of both left and right side control arms. One way to minimize poor suspension geometry designs is to use stiff anti-roll bars to reduce roll and suspension control arm movement.

## THE DIFFERENCES BETWEEN FRONT DRIVE, REAR DRIVE, AND ALL-WHEEL DRIVE

The basic goal, regardless of the drive wheel location, is to maximize tire traction at all four tire contact patches. This basically means there are more similarities than differences. Here is a list of the basic differences:

### Front-wheel Drive

About 20 years ago, I raced a front-wheel car for the first time. It was a Shelby CSX in the IMSA International Sedan Series. We used DOT race compound tires, and the engine produced about 250 horsepower with the car weighing in at about 2,500 pounds ready to race; front weight bias was about 61 percent. The car was built by Shelby, and the new owner wanted to make some significant changes after our initial testing, where we found the handling to be pretty dismal. It lacked overall grip, but was very hard to drive at the limit because the balance would change from understeer to oversteer and back several times in a corner.

After using computer software (then in its infancy) to analyze the suspension geometry, spring rates and bar rates, we made many changes. Realizing that the front tires were overworked, especially at the exit of a turn, where acceleration is crucial, I designed the suspension with an adjustable rear bar. There was inadequate room at the front for an adjustable bar. I calculated that the softest setting on the rear bar would have slight understeer, while the stiffest setting would have mild oversteer, with three middle settings for fine-tuning, On the softest setting, the car understeered mildly on the skid pad. After moving the bar a couple of notches stiffer, the handling balance was nearly perfect. Running on General Tires DOT race tires (not as sticky as some of the other tires, like the BFG) we managed to get a two-way skid

pad average of over 1.07 g on the skid pad, a phenomenal number in the late 1980s.

Front-drive cars typically have over 60 percent of the total car weight on the front axle. This means that the front tires not only provide most of the cornering power, but also must provide for acceleration and about 80 percent of the braking traction. On a front driver, the front tires do about 75 percent of all the work being done. For this reason, the rear tire should be about 20–25 percent narrower than the front tires, which is being done on many front drive cars where rules are open. If rules dictate that front and rear wheel and tire sizes must be the same, the rear anti-roll bar can be stiffened to the point that the inside rear tire lifts from the track surface. This often creates the perfect handling balance on a front driver.

- Suspension frequencies should be slightly higher at the front.
- If allowed, it's a good idea to move some heavy components, like the battery, to the rear of the car to improve weight distribution.
- Toe settings and camber settings will be different, with minimal toe-out at the front and less camber at the front compared to a rear drive.
- Less front camber allows the front tires to hook up better exiting corners.

### Rear-wheel Drive

- Suspension frequencies should be slightly higher at the rear.
- Rear drive cars usually don't need stiff rear anti-roll bars, in some cases no rear anti-roll bar.

The body roll on the Challenger is not affecting weight transfer, but the slight roll angle is small enough to minimize any negative effect of camber change on the front.
*Hotchkis Sport Suspension*

This Mitsubishi Evo all-wheel-drive car has a perfect setup for this corner. Note the inside front tire is just off the track surface, indicating a near ideal amount of roll couple. *Falken Tire*

- Rear drive cars with independent rear suspension will respond well to slight amounts of negative camber at the rear.
- Some rear drive cars respond well to a slight amount of rear toe-out, like the 1990s Nissan 350ZX.
- Most stock platform rear-drivers have too much front weight bias, so moving weight to the rear will help acceleration off the corners, or for drag racing.

### All-wheel Drive

- Suspension frequencies should be slightly higher at the front, unless weight bias is less than 50 percent at the front.
- All-wheel-drive cars usually respond well to stiff rear anti-roll bars, especially if the front weight bias is high.
- The all-wheel-drive car with heavy front weight bias works much like a front-drive car, except that a very stiff anti-roll bar is not necessary, since having both rear tire contact patches working on corner exit will improve exit acceleration.

ALL OTHER CRITERIA ARE THE SAME AMONG THE DIFFERENT DRIVE CONFIGURATONS!

## HANDLING TUNING MISTAKES

At the track, you're unloaded and ready to go for the first practice session. After the session is over, you feel lost because the handling is way off. You make changes that should help, but in the next session, the car feels even worse.

The same scenario continues for the remainder of the event, and you're very unhappy with the result. There is a good chance that one or more of the following is the culprit behind your situation.

Any one of these problems can be your undoing:

### Not Creating a Solid Baseline

One key to being fast and competitive is repeatability. You just cannot repeat results if you do not know where you started. A good chassis baseline is the one recommended by a prep shop. If you have the experience, create your own baseline. And best of all, if you have records from earlier races at the track you are going to, it gives you a head start. You should have the following: frame heights, crossweight percentage, rear and left-side weight percentages, all four tire circumferences, fuel load, gear ratio, spring rates, bar neutralized, shock valving, toe, rear alignment, pinion angle, Panhard bar height or Watt's linkage settings, and any other setting affecting the handling.

### Preparing the Car at the Track

This happens too often. You run out of time or have inadequate help before an event, so you end up preparing the car at the track, or at least finishing the job there. It is very difficult to create a good setup at the track. It is easier and much more effective in the garage. Track time is expensive for a test day. Wasting that time is not effective. And if you're prepping your car at a race, forget any chance of a good result.

The Challenger and the Corvette are showing good form through an esse section, indication little body roll and good transitional handling characteristics, a function of a well-designed and tested suspension package for both cars. *Hotchkis Sport Suspension*

## Not Taking Tire Temperatures

Tire temperatures are your link to what goes on between the tire contact patch and the track surface. I find it difficult to make sound tuning decisions without tire temps. Tire temperatures should be taken religiously every time the car comes in after a run on the track.

## Not Taking Segment Times

Time around the track is gained in very small increments. Chassis adjustments can make a car faster (or slower) around the track, but may cost time in certain areas of the racetrack. Knowing this can add to the data available for you to make sound tuning choices. The only way to accomplish this is to record times in several segments of the racetrack. You don't need to take times in every segment on every lap, but taking segments at various points for each session will prove very valuable, especially in testing.

## Crossweight Is Off

Crossweight, the measure of right-front and left-rear combined weight vs. total car weight (both with driver) is a useful tuning tool. In road racing or autocrossing situations, excessive crossweight will help handling in one direction but hurt in the other—and it hurts more one way than it helps the other way. Crossweight should be set at 50 percent and never less than 49.5 percent or more than 50.5 percent.

## Not Keeping Records

This may be the most costly sin of all. There is just too much data to keep track of without writing everything down in an organized way. Even if you have a good setup, without records you will be unable to repeat the setup without going through the complete process all over again. The most important time to record records is back in the shop after a race. If you

have a good race setup, this will tell you how to get back to the setup the next time you race at that track under similar circumstances. And if the results were not so good, at least you know you need to do something different.

## Listening to Too Much Advice

Everyone is a setup expert, so most people would have you believe. To achieve success it is imperative that you learn enough to make your own tuning decisions within your own team. Listening to advice from others is one thing, putting it to use is another. Even if the person offering advice is very knowledgeable, that person likely does not know your situation, preferences, resources, or needs. It's difficult to give advice that is useful. And most often, the person offering advice is less knowledgeable than you are, and usually only knows a couple of things that could cure your perceived problem.

## Not Creating a Game Plan

Any plan is better than no plan at all. Take the time to create a game plan for each event, beginning with your realistic objectives, maintenance schedules, testing, and strategy. And remember that part of a good game plan is the flexibility to alter the plan as needed. Usually, no plan equals no result.

## Not Determining Exactly Where the Problem Begins

A handling problem can occur anywhere on the track. Is it corner entry, mid-turn, or corner exit? Or does it happen everywhere? If a problem occurs in one place, does it result in a different problem someplace else? The classic example of this is corner entry understeer that a driver overcompensates for, and at the exit of the corner, creates an oversteer condition. The driver says the car is oversteering, but the real problem is the corner entry push. Adjusting for the oversteer will make the problem worse.

## Having a Suspension Bind

Suspension binds create an inconsistent handling situation. If a bind is present, it is just about impossible to tune the suspension. If the car does not respond to changes the way you think it should, check for bind in the suspension. And checking for binds should be part of your routine setup process.

## Having a Dead Shock

A bad shock can be very difficult to feel. Check the shocks if you cannot get the chassis tuned effectively. Feel for a dead spot or lack of resistance in both rebound and compression.

## Too Aggressive Setup for Driver Experience

Often, the fastest setup for a given car is too aggressive for a driver without some experience. When the suspension is too stiff, especially the shock valving, it is difficult for the driver to feel what the chassis is doing. The car reacts too quickly for the driver to sense what is occurring. Softer springs and shocks, while slower for the experienced driver, may be faster for the inexperienced driver.

## Making Corner Weight Adjustments at One Corner Only

To adjust corner weight percentage, you must change ride height. Suspension geometry is designed to work best at a certain ride height and angle. Changing the frame height can alter the suspension geometry in a negative manner. Making one big change at one corner can cause this to happen. The trick is to make small changes at all four corners. Instead of putting a turn in the right front, put a quarter turn in the right front and left rear, and take a quarter turn out of the left front and right rear.

## Trying to Cure Handling Problems with Only One Element

Any handling problem can be changed by adjusting several different parts on a car. It is ineffective to use only one or two items to affect the handling. Often, engineers—shock, tire, spring, etc.—will try to cure a problem by using what they know best. This is often not the most effective way to do things. It is important to look at the entire system as a whole, then make changes that suit the system best and offer the most favorable compromise.

## Making More than One Change at a Time

It is always best to make only one change at a time. Making more than one change can prove difficult to analyze. Which change helped; did one change actually hurt?

## Moving Too Far Away from Recommended Ride Heights

This can cause binding in the suspension or at a minimum cause undesirable suspension geometry.

## Inaccuracy in Measurements

As bad as not keeping records in the first place is recording inaccurate measurements. This can lead to all kinds of problems.

## Inconsistent Fuel Load

Changing fuel load will always be a setup and tuning problem. As fuel is burned off, handling will change. If you do not tune at a constant fuel load, your data will be inaccurate and the results misleading. No more than a two-gallon fluctuation is acceptable. One gallon is a better mark.

Make one change, then test the change. *Progress Technology*

### Crew/Driver Communications

If the crew and/or driver are not sure of the concepts of tuning and clear about the language, all sorts of problems can occur. Everyone on the team needs to be on the same page.

### Driver Overdriving

If a driver is overdriving the track or setup, most of the data, whether from the driver or tire temperatures, will be less than accurate. Overdriving not only abuses the tires but also masks real handling problems. At the opposite end of the spectrum is the driver under-driving the car. If the tires lack adequate heat for maximum traction, it is nearly impossible to determine the causes of handling problems. Tires, especially purpose-built race tires need heat. The traction levels can be awful until heat is in the tire treads. Many drivers have spun out on warm up laps due to this. It is important to get tires up to optimum temps quickly.

### Making Changes That Are Too Big

If a change is too big, you can cause a handling problem that is worse than the one you already have. On the other hand, a change that is too small can be difficult to detect by the driver or the stop watch. Big changes would be more than two numbers on shock valving, more than 15 percent in spring or bar rate, more than a ¼ inch in ride height.

### Not Understanding the Whole System

Understanding the whole system is very important. The key is to understand how any change affects the tire contact load and traction. Always thinking in terms of tire contact patch load and traction will help you focus on making the best change possible for the situation.

### Chasing Changing Track Conditions

Track conditions constantly change. The car may get faster during the day even though the lap times are slower. The track may be slowing even faster than the car is getting faster. If in doubt, return to the starting setup to see how the track has changed.

### Chasing Old Tires

At some point, tires get too hard to be fast. There is a point that no matter what you do the car will not get faster. Chasing an old set of tires is ineffective.

This Camaro has near perfect ride height for a track day car. Any lower and the suspension would bottom out, causing handling problems, and the chassis could bottom on the road surface. *Hotchkis Sport Suspension*

Autocrossing requires a stiffer, more aggressive setup than a road race track setup since everything happens very quickly and transitions are much more abrupt. Tire overheating is not an issue unless the driver overdrives the car. *Hotchkis Sport Suspension*

Drifting is an extreme activity from a setup perspective. It's not covered here because it requires a setup and a driving technique that requires reducing traction at the rear, not maximizing overall tire traction. *Falken Tire*

# Chapter 9
# Track Driving Techniques

**O**ften overlooked as a handling factor, the driver is actually one of the biggest factors affecting handling balance. The driver influences weight transfer by how and when the controls are utilized. If a car is traveling at a steady speed in a straight line, there is no weight transfer. But when the driver begins to use the brakes, apply the throttle, or turn the steering wheel, weight transfer begins to occur. And how quickly the driver applies the throttle or brake, or turns the steering wheel affects how quickly weight transfer happens. So the driver controls when weight transfer begins and affects how fast it takes place. And weight transfer affects traction and roll couple distribution or handling balance. So how well the driver manipulates the controls determines how well the driver is managing tire traction.

Being a crew chief or engineer on an endurance race team offers insights into how the drivers affect handling, and how different one driver's approach can be compared to another. Data logging has helped determine what is really going on

when one driver says the car is oversteering at a given spot while another driver insists the car is understeering at the same spot. The difficulty is that they could both be correct. With data logging, we can see that one driver is using the controls differently, causing a slight push while the control use of the other driver is causing a slightly loose condition. This usually means that the car has a very good setup.

Here's another example. In her first season in NASCAR, IndyCar Series star Danica Patrick has been struggling with consistency. It's not her driving or her ability to drive at the limit. It comes down to a radically different platform requiring a very different driving style than the open-wheel Indy cars she is used to. First, the tires and tire loading changes due to weight transfer require different driving techniques. And the radically changing weight from diminishing fuel loads changes the weight balance during a run, and that is where she is struggling the most. An Indy car driver has a stable platform where the reduction

*Toyo Tire USA*

The driver has a much greater influence on handling than most people realize. When and how the controls are used makes a dramatic difference in both balance and lap times. *Falken Tire*

This driver has timed his turn-in around the pylon perfectly. A straight-line slalom is a great test for the driver as well as the responsiveness of the suspension. *Hotchkis Sport Suspension*

of weight from fuel usage is better balanced front to rear during a run. The loss of over 100 pounds over the rear of a NASCAR stock car during a run requires the driver to constantly change how the controls are being used. This is not an easy concept to adapt to when you are used to driving much faster cars that are also more consistent as fuel loads diminish. How well a driver can adapt to this is a big factor in success on the racetrack.

Small changes in steering wheel angle and how fast the driver rotates the wheel, how hard and quickly the brake pedal is applied, and how smoothly power is applied can make a big difference in handling balance, lap times, and, over the course of a race or run, how well tires are managed. Smooth, consistent motions relative to control use will have a very different effect on the platform balance and tire traction compared to rapid and abrupt control inputs.

While the driver must learn to set the car up to optimize overall traction, the driver must also learn what the car needs to get around the racetrack quickly. Many people can tune a piano. Few can regularly provide virtuoso performances.

## HOW THE DRIVER AFFECTS HANDLING
### Handling Ailments: Car or Driver?

During qualifying, a driver picks up a considerable push in mid-turn after about three quick laps. He comes into the pits for an adjustment. The crew stiffens the rear anti-roll bar and he goes back out. On his first lap at speed, the car gets real loose going into turn one. He nearly spins, but he manages to get the car gathered up. He goes back into the pits for another change, this time stiffening the front anti-roll bar. The loose condition disappears going into the turn on cool tires, but the push is worse than ever in mid-turn after he gets heat into the rubber. He comes back in, confused about what to do next.

This driver probably did not consider all of the options available when the mid-turn push was first encountered. One of the most likely causes is the driver. Driver error should always be considered when handling problems crop up. There are several items to consider when analyzing handling problems. The first is to confirm or eliminate the driver as a possible cause. Keep in mind, the driver influences weight transfer and tire traction at each corner of the car in a variety of situations. If the driver is too hard on the throttle, he can cause either a push or a loose condition, depending on what he does with the throttle pedal and when. How and when the driver uses any of the controls will often cause or cure a perceived handling problem.

### How a Driver Can Cause a Handling Problem Entering a Turn

The opening scenario is common. But how does it happen? It's incredibly easy for a driver to cause this problem. If the driver comes into the corner too hot under hard braking, and attempts to rotate the car while applying too much brake pedal pressure, then a significant push is created. Ironically, it can also cause the car to get loose. If the car has too much brake bias to the rear, a loose situation can result under heavy braking while steering; too much front bias and the situation reverses. A slight roll couple bias can have the same effect. Too much front roll couple causes a push, too much rear will create a loose situation.

The overriding factor here is the driver. If the driver brakes too hard and tries to rotate the car (more steering wheel lock applied by the driver while braking), the car will have a handling problem just like the one described in the opening scene. The situation may not appear again until the tires get hot. This will typically cause the car to push since the front tires may be overheating due to heavy braking going into the corners. The situation will only get worse as the tires get hotter and begin to wear.

Even if a car is perfectly neutral, the driver can cause a handling problem by making the steering motion too quickly or abruptly. Jerking the steering wheel can cause the front tire slip angles to increase suddenly relative to the rear tire slip angles, causing a push to begin, which can linger even though the rear tire slip angles eventually catch up to the front slip angles.

While Tanner Foust is drifting this car on purpose, this is an extreme loose condition or oversteer. While the handling balance of the car can cause this, so can the driver. A skilled driver can make a car with basic understeer slide sideways like this by manipulating the controls at the perfect instant. *Toyo Tire USA*

The corner exit is less critical, but still important. The key is maximum acceleration with no wheelspin. *Hotchkis Sport Suspension*

## How a Driver Can Cause a Handling Problem While Exiting a Turn

Corner exit handling problems can also be driver-caused. The most common situation is wheelspin exiting a turn. This is almost always caused by the driver slamming the throttle pedal too quickly. More crossweight may reduce this on an oval, but on a road course, it's the driver that has considerable influence over the situation. Just like the entry of a turn, the same action by the driver could cause the exact opposite problem. A push at the exit of the turn can also be driver-induced simply by accelerating too hard with too much steering lock. If the relative amount of drive torque available is too little to cause wheelspin, the weight transfer due to acceleration can increase rear tire traction while reducing front tire traction. This change in balance often causes a push at the exit of a turn when wheelspin is not likely to occur. In each case, the driver is misusing the controls, which upsets the handling balance.

## Attempting to Fix Driver-Induced Handling Problems with Setup Changes

The temptation for a driver is always to "fix" the problem by changing the setup of the car. Drivers, or crew chiefs for that matter, rarely look to the driver as the cause of a handling problem. A driver is the cause more often than not of these types of handling problems, especially if the driver is inexperienced, new to a given car or class, or new to a given racetrack. It is also likely if the driver is not sensitive to changing traction as the track conditions change or tire grip diminishes.

Attempting to change the setup to cure driver-induced handling ills will likely cause more handling ills and hurt overall car performance. For example, if the car is loose at the exit because of wheelspin, more crossweight may help. But that may cause a push going into the turns. And even if the increased crossweight reduces or eliminates the wheelspin, the car may now push at the exit also. The example in the opening scenario indicates what could happen at the turn entry. There are many other possibilities! Anytime a car is adjusted to fix a driver-caused handling problem, some other problem will occur, usually creating a more serious situation. To achieve the best possible, fastest setup requires that driver errors be minimized, especially during transitional periods such as entering and exiting corners. If the driver continues to upset the delicate balance of the car during these crucial phases of transition, handling problems will persist.

## How to Cure Driver-Induced Handling Problems

The first step in curing driver-induced handling ills is to recognize that the driver may be the cause of the problem. This can be very difficult for two reasons. First, handling problems can be easily masked since several different scenarios can be the cause for a given problem. Second, it can be difficult for drivers to have the insight and honesty needed to look within for the problem. It takes courage and commitment to confront yourself and your ego to seek the truth. There are several clues to help determine whether the car or the driver is the root of the problem.

- If the problem is inconsistent, it is most likely driver-induced.
- If a problem occurs at every similar type of turn, it is most likely, but not always, setup related.
- On road courses, if a problem occurs on either left or right turns only, it is likely setup related.
- If the problem occurs at one turn only or one segment of a turn, it is likely driver-induced.

In the rain, with greatly reduced traction, the driver can easily influence handling balance. The driver must be very smooth and the suspension compliant to be quick in the rain. *Falken Tire*

The more powerful the car and the tighter the corner, the more likely that wheelspin will be a problem. This situation requires a later apex. *Falken Tire*

With adequate traction, the driver can accelerate at full throttle before the apex is reached.

This photo shows what happens with even slight wheel lock-up at the entry of a corner.

## IMPROVING YOUR DRIVING TECHNIQUE

Driver control errors cause handling problems. These errors fall into two categories, all occurring during transitions. The first is abrupt control responses. Jerking the steering wheel, hitting the brake pedal too hard, or nailing the throttle to the floor too quickly are the usual problems. Second, the timing of control use may be off. Turning the steering wheel too soon or too late going into a turn can upset the car, causing problems. The same applies to the brake and throttle pedals. Smooth movements of the controls timed perfectly will eliminate most of the driver-induced handling problems.

Here are some examples. Turning the steering wheel too quickly at the entry to a turn can cause a push or loose condition as previously described. This relates closely to the use of the brakes in unison with steering. If the steering wheel is turned too quickly while the brakes are applied too much going into a turn, the tires will be overloaded. The tires can steer and decelerate the car at the same time, but only up to a point. The combination of brake and steering cannot exceed the limits of total tire traction. The tires create only so much traction regardless of direction (accelerate or brake, plus turn). The combination can go right to the traction limit, but not exceed it. All of the traction can be used to turn, or to brake, or some combination of the two. If the limit is exceeded, the tires will slide, usually at one end of the car before the other (front tires first is a push or understeer condition).

The driver is in complete control of this. More steering means less brake; more brake means less steering. If you need to turn the wheel while braking at the limits of tire traction, the tires cannot do the job. To steer requires less traction to be used for braking. The more steering required, the less braking you can use. If all the traction is needed for turning, then no braking can be used, and vice versa.

The same situation applies to the corner exit. More traction for acceleration requires less steering lock by the driver. Maximum traction efficiency requires you to stay on the limit of the traction circle. If you go over the limit of the traction circle by asking the tires to do more work than they can, a handling problem will occur.

Think of the throttle and brake pedals as being attached to the steering wheel. More pressure on the pedal means less steering lock. More steering lock means less pressure on the pedals. Too much steering or too much pedal pressure causes tire traction limits to be exceeded.

As you enter a turn under braking, you must ease off the brake pedal in order to stay within the limits of traction. At some point in the turn, all of the traction must be used for cornering, so the brakes are released and the car balanced with the throttle (without acceleration). At the exit of a turn, to facilitate acceleration down the straights, the steering wheel must be unwound. If it is not, a handling problem, caused by the driver, will occur. The big question is finding the balance between pedal application and steering wheel lock angle. It's like walking a tightrope. Too much of either will cause the fine balance to be lost and the car will fall off the desired path. Too little will be slow. Learning to keep the car balanced on the edge of traction is the key to being a fast race driver.

Finally, timing of control use is crucial for fast driving. Turning in too early can require using more steering lock midway into a turn. This should require a reduction in braking force, but then you may enter the corner with too much speed. This circumstance may also alter your line around the corner. Braking too late, turning in too late, not rotating the car at the best place on the track can force you to slow the car to avert disaster. Timing can be thrown off if control movements are too slow. The combination of smooth control use, perfect balance between pedal and steering inputs, and precise timing make driving a race car an art form. Being off by 5 degrees of steering wheel angle, 10 pounds on brake pedal pressure, or a tenth of a second on timing can cost valuable hundredths of a second on the racetrack. True speed is found by perfecting your skills in these areas.

Smaller, more nimble cars can be driven more aggressively on a tight autocross course. *Toyo Tire USA/David Cosseboom GotCone.com*

These cars are on different exit lines. The rear car is using less steering lock, which reduces tire scrub and allows more speed and acceleration. Another benefit in a race is keeping the tires slightly cooler, which means better grip toward the end of the event.

Too much throttle at the exit with too much steering lock can cause a quick spin.

The silver car following the blue WRX has kept a tighter line in the big sweeper the cars are exiting. These cars do not need to brake for the following right hand turn. The WRX is using less total steering input and keeping the chassis freer and carrying more speed.

## THE OVERALL GOAL

It is important to keep in mind that the singular goal is to get around the racetrack as fast as possible, whether for a single lap or an entire race. Race car dynamics relate ultimately to tire traction at the tire contact patch. Optimizing traction on the complete car means faster lap times. We can do this by manipulating the chassis components and the driver's steering, braking, and accelerator inputs. Not only does the driver operate the controls, but the driver's input concerning what the car is doing at specific points on the racetrack plays a paramount role in success. The team doing the best job of this will be in the top five. From there, tactics, strategy, execution, and maybe a little luck will determine the winner.

## BASIC CORNERING THEORY FOR THE TRACK

Entire books exist covering this topic, but here are four basic principles to get you going in the right direction. While it is crucial to drive the corners as close to the limit as possible, the real goal and the overriding factor for the best (and fastest) way to get around the track is to find the best compromises allowing you to accelerate, preferably at full throttle, the maximum amount of time during a lap. While both braking and steering are an absolute necessity, both actually slow the car, so spending the least amount of time steering and braking and the most time accelerating is the key to fast lap times.

## 1. Turn the Steering as Little as Possible While Cornering

The act of steering scrubs off speed. For this reason, spend as little time as possible steering. And turn the steering wheel as little as possible to get through a corner. This is an "AREA UNDER THE CURVE" exercise. If you plot on a graph the steering angle of the steering wheel vs. the time spent turning the steering wheel, the driver with the least area under the curve is the fastest. This requires scribing the largest arc possible through a corner. A line starting from the outside edge of the track, apexing at the geometric center of the corner on the inside of the track, and exiting to the outside edge of the track will accomplish this as long as the arc is smooth. Steering corrections, while necessary at times, add to the area under the curve and cost time.

## 2. Alter Your Line If You Encounter Corner Exit Wheelspin

The goal is to get back on full power as early as possible exiting a corner. Some corners are flat out, allowing full throttle throughout, but most corners require braking to negotiate the turn. But getting back on full power as quickly as possible is the key to fast laps. If full throttle application induces wheelspin, alter your line so that you can unwind the steering earlier in the exit phase of the corner. This allows the tires to use more traction capacity for acceleration. This line requires a later turn-in (meaning more steering angle) and a later apex but an earlier throttle application to full power and maximum acceleration.

### 3. Use Limit Braking with Caution

Braking at the limits of tire traction, also called threshold braking, is important for fast lap times, but it can cause problems at corner turn-in. Keep the traction circle theory in mind. As you reach the turn-in point, ease off the brakes as you begin to steer. More steering means less braking. You should be braking for a slow corner about ⅓ of the way into the turn for maximum tire traction utilization. But you must find the fine balance between steering and braking to take advantage of the tire's maximum traction. Too much steering for the amount of braking will cause a handling problem, scrubbing off speed and overheating the tires at the minimum or resulting in an off track excursion (or crash) at worst.

### 4. Control Use: Smooth vs. Abrupt

Smoothness counts. Abrupt use of the controls can initiate handling problems, overheat tires, and accelerate wear. It is almost always slower. There are rare cases where abrupt control inputs can be used to coax the car into a desired behavior, but if such a tactic works, then the car's setup needs to be addressed. Long term abrupt control use destroys tires quickly and costs time in any event lasting longer than a single lap.

Abrupt steering input can cause tire slip angles to increase too quickly, overloading the tires, and can cause the slip angles to be higher than necessary, causing scrub, heat buildup, and accelerated tire wear. Too abrupt on the throttle can cause wheelspin. And an abrupt application of the brakes can cause wheel lockup and force forward weight transfer to take place too quickly, overloading the front tires at the turn-in to a corner.

So what is smooth? That's tough to define! The best advice is to try using the controls more slowly. You may not be able to tell when you are using the controls too quickly, but you will know when you are using them too slowly. Slow down control movements until they feel too slow.

## WHEN YOU DRIVE, WHERE YOU LOOK IS WHERE YOU GO

It's your first time trial event and the adrenaline is flowing like crazy. You start to work up to speed, but the feeling of speed is nearly overwhelming to you as you start to go faster. You're having trouble staying ahead of the car and the feeling is just a little frightening. You realize that you are following another car fairly closely, and are focused on his rear bumper. You look past the car ahead and suddenly the anxiety diminishes. By looking farther down the track, you relax and things are happening slower. The driving is more fun and is actually much safer. And now you start to go faster than ever without the same level of stress.

This scene is common. Where you look determines nearly every aspect of your driving: speed, comfort, style, and safety. But it is important to use your eyes effectively to become a better driver and to go faster as well. Visual fields are one of the most important areas of attention for any

This American Iron Class Mustang has entered the corner too fast, resulting in tire lock-up in the right front (unloaded tire) at turn-in.

The consequence is a loss of front tire total traction resulting in understeer and a quick trip into the grass.

Had the driver eased of the brakes sooner, traction would have improved and the car may have stayed on the track. Time would still be lost, but much less and possible tire damage would be reduced

In a spec class like this National Spec Miata Action, the difference is in small setup and tuning changes—the driver who uses the least amount of steering and the most throttle for the duration of the event will often come home in front. *Toyo Tire USA/Mark Weber*

driver, but especially for the competition driver. What you see determines how you implement and modify your game plan. If you fail to see something important, it can cause problems. Knowing where to look and what to look for is crucial for success, as well as safety, in all forms of driving.

## VISUAL FIELDS

Visual fields are simply where you look and what your eyes are taking in. Most of the data you gather for decision making in a race car is taken in visually. Your visual field could be the dashboard, down the road 300 yards, into a corner, a billboard, or anywhere you look. A short visual field limits data gathering, while a long visual field promotes greater data intake. The data you gather is needed to make decisions. "Where do I apply the brakes? When do I turn the steering wheel, and how much? What are the other cars doing?" Each of these questions and dozens of others are answered by visual data you take in while on the track. If the visual data you take in is faulty, inaccurate or incomplete, the result will be lost time on the track and much greater risk on the highway. You'll either be too slow or too scared.

## FOCAL POINTS

Your focal point determines what your visual field encompasses. Try this exercise right now. Focus on the page you are now reading. Don't change your focal point, but notice what is in your peripheral visual field. What you see is limited, so the data you can gather from your visual field is limited. Now focus on an object several feet away. Do the same thing with your peripheral vision. You can take in more data. Try this on objects even farther away. As your focal point moves out away from you, your ability to gather important data improves. Within reason, the longer your focal point, the larger your visual field and the more data you can take in with your eyes. What you focus your eyes on is very important.

Uphill exits transfer weight to the rear tires and allow much more throttle application much sooner in the exit zone of a corner. *Hotchkis Sport Suspension*

## THE CRYSTAL BALL

Your visual field is like a crystal ball. It allows you to take a look into the future. And the future can keep you ahead of the competition. For example, at 130 miles per hour, you are traveling at about 200 feet per second. If you look 200 feet ahead, you have a one second look at what will occur in 200 feet. But if you look at the bumper of the car just ahead, you have only 1/10 second look into the future.

During the time you give yourself with your visual field, there are three important factors to process. First, that is the time you have to implement your plan. Second, it is the time you have to plan tactics based on the cars around you. Third, it is the most amount of time you have to take evasive action in an emergency. You may have less time if the situation occurs within your visual field closer to you. Let's look at these more closely.

## Your Plan

Whether you realize it or not, you have a plan for getting around a racetrack or down the highway. You must "plan" when you will turn the steering wheel, when to brake, and when to use the throttle. Your visual field determines how far your plan reaches and how much time you have to implement the plan. If your visual field encompasses 100 feet in front of you, your plan for using the controls to position the car and control its speed extends 100 feet, and the time you have to implement the plan is determined by the speed of the vehicle. *For all practical purposes, your plan ends where your visual field ends.* To get through a corner effectively, you need a plan to get you completely through a corner. And that requires a visual field that stretches through the corner. A big visual field will allow you to see the path you want to drive and make smooth transitions on and off the controls. A short visual field, even if it shifts, does not allow you to see the big view, so you are forced to make several smaller plans, leaving little time to implement the plan and requiring you to react to, rather than anticipate, situations. This forces more abrupt transitions, and can cause you to lose speed.

## Tactics

Your visual field will affect your ability to create and implement tactics. The more you are forced to react to situations, the greater your *disadvantage* becomes. Larger visual fields allow you to anticipate tactical situations earlier in the majority of situations. If you count on reacting to situations, you will lose just about every time. If you give yourself time to anticipate the situation, whether you are attacking or defending, you will have a higher likelihood of success.

## Avoiding Situations and Crashes

While a crash can happen directly in front of you, leaving no time to react, your best chance for avoiding the situation is a large visual field. The large visual field buys you time to avoid situations a little ways down the track.

# WHAT TO LOOK AT

Visual fields should always be dynamic—that is, always moving and changing. It is ineffective to focus on a marker or object 300 feet down the road, and maintain focus on that object until you pass. The effective way to use visual fields is to constantly change them. Keep your eyes moving. For example, as you approach a corner, your eyes may sweep through the braking zone, and then through the corner to the exit before moving back to your braking point and the path you plan to drive at the entry to the turn. During this time, you may also glance at the mirror or use your peripheral vision to check on the position of other cars.

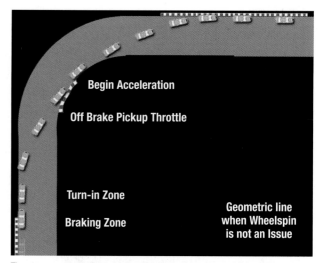

The orange cars track the racing line that allows the most speed through the corner. This line is best for flat-out corners or any time that full power can be applied without wheelspin.

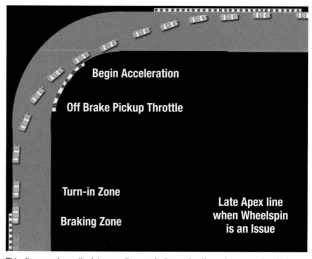

This diagram shows the late apex line used when going through a corner in which wheelspin is likely to occur. This line is often used on autocross courses, in wet weather conditions, and by high-powered vehicles without downforce.

At different times, the visual priorities will change depending on your position on the track, the situation in a race, and other circumstances. It is best if you have an idea of where you need to shift your visual field at various points around the racetrack, or in various situations.

## Road Signs

All racetracks and all roads have reference points of some type. These points can be anything: marks on the racetrack, cracks, marks on the walls, poles, etc. Use reference points to help you create and maintain your plan. Be sure to use permanent markers, not ones that can move.

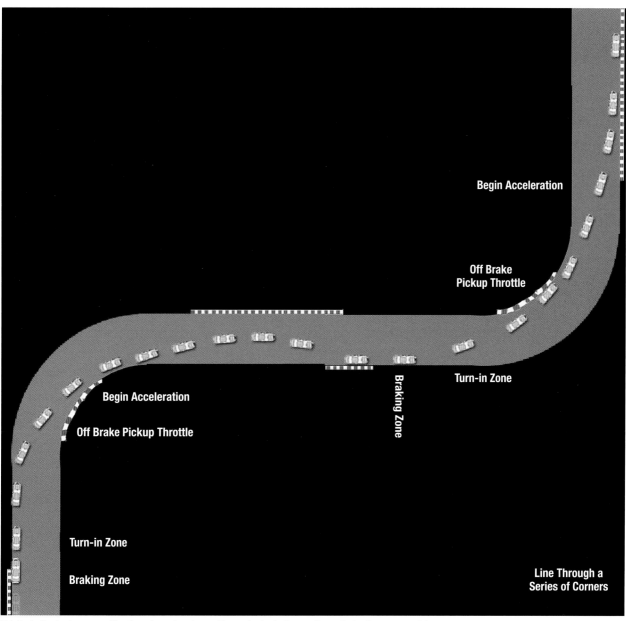

**Begin Acceleration**

**Off Brake Pickup Throttle**

**Turn-in Zone**

**Braking Zone**

**Begin Acceleration**

**Off Brake Pickup Throttle**

**Turn-in Zone**

**Braking Zone**

**Line Through a Series of Corners**

This illustration tracks a general line through a series of turns. Always plan for the last turn in a series leading onto a straightaway.

## Under Braking

As you approach the braking area, you should look all the way through the braking zone into the corner so that your plan is as complete as possible. Then shift your visual focus to the braking point, and allow your eyes to follow your desired path through the braking zone. As the brakes are applied, your visual field should shift to the corner, so that you have a clear mental picture of your desired path into and through the corner.

## Going into a Corner

As you go into the corner, you should have already looked completely through the turn; then you can shorten your visual field for specific reference points. Once into the corner, your visual field should move to the exit.

## Exiting a Corner

You must see out of the corner as early as possible so that you can unwind the steering and feed in throttle to maximize acceleration. This is probably the most important phase of the corner, and your visual focus is important. It is best to extend your visual field out of the corner as early as possible. Once your path is determined on the exit, you can check the mirrors or gauges as you enter the straight.

## Invisible Corners

In many cases, especially on road courses, you will encounter physical obstacles which impair your vision or create a blind cornering situation. In these cases, you need to have experience well below the limits of traction through those areas in order to drive them effectively. With experience, you will be able to get up to the limit. This process allows you to see "through" the blind spot as if it were not there. You are actually fooling your mind into believing that you actually see through the blind area. The risk is higher—since you cannot see developing trouble and you cannot plan tactics in such an area—but you can drive to the limits using this technique. The key is to practice at low speed, gradually build speed as confidence and experience increase, then start to approach the corner near or at the limits.

## Summary

Most of the data you accumulate is visual. A larger visual field will allow you to take in more information, and give you more time to process it. Short visual fields limit data and force the driver to react instead of anticipate. Anticipation of control usage allows you to drive more smoothly and precisely. To become a proficient driver, you should work on making the best use of your visual field. Keep it long and moving. This will buy you time, improve your performance, and make all forms of driving safer.

## DRIVING A LAP VS. A RACE

Many events use a format where one timed lap is the basis for results. Time trials, time attacks, autocrosses, and even qualifying for a road race are included in this list. In a road race, the driver must find a setup and a driving style that manages the tires for the duration. As discussed earlier, this is an "area under the curve" situation. The setup of the car and the technique of the driver must work in unison to manage the tires, so that at the end of the race the tires are still creating near maximum traction. Some setups and driving techniques cause extensive tire wear early in the race. This can cause tire degradation too quickly, causing the tires to "go off" before the end of the race. Many races are lost due to this.

But where the above can cost a team a race over several laps, the exact opposite is true for a single lap qualifier or run for time. A more aggressive setup and driving style can make a car faster for a single lap. More camber, different tire pressures, a setup with slightly more oversteer, and more aggressive driving can be faster for a single lap. Lighter fuel loads mean a different setup can be used and overheating the tires is rarely an issue for a one-lap run. And an astute driver can even use different tactics relative to driving the track. Very aggressive driving on a warm up lap can put heat in the tires for the flying lap. A driver can even alter lines to take advantage of the track configuration.

Blind corners require the driver to "see" what is not visible in the mind's eye. Use visualization techniques for practice. *Falken Tire*

TRACK DRIVING TECHNIQUE

Endurance racing presents great challenges to the driver. Not only do long-distance endurance races often present changing conditions—wet vs. dry, day vs. night—the driver must be adaptable enough to push the car to its limits when fast lap times are needed or show the consistency, concentration, and patience required to run a steady pace while minimizing tire and car wear. *Falken Tire*

My home track is Willow Springs International Raceway in California. The last turn exiting onto the straight is a right-hander, but turn one at the far end of the straight is a left-hander. This necessitates moving across the track to set up for turn one. Many drivers make the move across the track quickly, reaching the right edge of the track well before the start/finish line, which is about ⅔ of the way down the straight. Doing this early causes tire scrub sooner. This reduces acceleration very slightly. Moving over later also scrubs speed, but this happens at higher speeds and minimizes the loss of acceleration. But I always took this a step further. When I knew I was on a good lap, I would wait until I was past the start/finish line before moving across the track. The lateral move across the track adds about 50 feet to the lap distance. At an average straightaway speed from the exit of turn 9 (a high speed corner) to the entry of turn 1 (a medium speed corner) of 100 miles per hour (147 feet/second), not traversing that extra 50 feet saves about ³⁄₁₀ of a second on that lap. Of course it hurts the following lap, but if you only need a single lap, so what?

So if you compete in a situation where a single lap means everything, use a setup and driving style that takes that fact into account. And always look for little tricks that give you an "unfair advantage."

## OTHER UNIQUE SITUATIONS—THE LAUNCH

If you drag race or autocross, the launch is crucial. Heat in the tires is important, as are debris-free tire treads. The launch itself requires the perfect balance between engine RPM, torque, and traction. This takes practice, but one fact is little known. What is the optimum amount of wheelspin for maximum acceleration off the line? Most would say no wheelspin, but they would be wrong. Everyone has seen smoky burnouts where the car is barely moving and the tires are billowing clouds of smoke. This is approaching 100 percent wheelspin, meaning that the car is not moving. Almost any car can do this on ice. Zero percent wheelspin means the car is moving exactly the distance of one tire circumference for every revolution of the tire tread.

In the early days of drag racing, some Cal Tech rocket science students calculated that the fastest possible quarter-mile elapsed time was around 9 seconds, the time that exactly 1 g acceleration would allow. They argued that 1 g of acceleration would require perfect adhesion of the tire to the track surface, which would require a coefficient of friction of one. They were proven wrong in short order when dragsters in the mid-1950s were setting ETs faster than predicted. It turns out that tires on asphalt or concrete can easily exceed a coefficient of friction of one.

And it turns out that the highest possible coefficient occurs within a very small range of tire slippage, or wheelspin. Within the range of 3 to 6 percent slippage is where optimum traction occurs, so a little wheelspin is needed for maximum acceleration from a drag racing or autocrossing launch.

If we consider the launch to occur over the first 100 feet and the tire circumference is exactly 6.667 feet, it will take 15 revolutions of the tire to travel 100 feet with zero percent wheelspin. But for optimum acceleration the drive tires will actually rotate between 15.45 and 15.90 revolutions. That's not much wheelspin, but it works, and it takes considerable skill and practice to be able to launch a car with that precise amount of wheelspin. No one said this is easy.

One more key to optimum launches is knowing where to line up. For drag racing, line up where you think the most traction will be for the launch, then drive a straight line path down the track. Lateral movement adds to the ET. For autocrossing, line up at the edge that sets you up for the first turn. Moving across the course to set up for the first turn will add time to your run.

As you can see from this chapter, the driver plays a crucial role in handling as well as overall success in competition. While the driver should be the easiest element on a car to adjust, drivers are rarely that easy to tune. Egos are hard to read and work with. For that reason, most skilled drivers leave their egos behind. A driver with a big ego is like trying to tune tires covered with grease. Progress is hard to gauge.

Drag races are won on the line with just enough wheelspin to generate maximum traction. After the launch, minimal steering and going straight down the track take priority.
*Hotchkis Sport Suspension*

# Chapter 10
# Track Driving Overview

In today's crowded world, driving near the limits of a car's potential is both foolhardy and dangerous, except on a track. And there are several ways you can do that, from mild to wild, and many are surprisingly inexpensive. Different clubs and types of events are available to suit individual needs, desires, and goals. There are many options, so fire up the web browser and start searching. Here's an overview.

## DRAG RACING

One of the easiest forms of motorsport to jump into is drag racing. The process is simple to understand, procedures are easy, and the skills required to have fun are minimal. Car setup is unnecessary for entry-level stock classes. On one hand, drag racing at the entry level is cheap. On the other, it can cost $50,000 to build a 10-second quarter-mile machine. The fun level of quarter-mile runs is high, but the track time is minimal and often the wait between runs can be very long. No license beyond a driver's license is needed to compete and entry fees are small.

## AUTOCROSS/SOLO II

Here is another form of motorsport that is very easy to get involved in and have a lot of fun. An autocross or Solo II is a mini road course setup, most often laid out in a parking lot with orange traffic cones. Speeds are low, and while sticky tires will make your ride faster, they are not required for giving autocrossing a try. If you get serious about autocrossing in a prepared class, car modifications to your daily driver can range up to several thousand dollars, but very limited modifications are allowed in the stock classes. Runs last about a minute and you normally get three or four in an afternoon. Expect to spend a couple hours working the course while other classes compete. It's all part of the fun. Autocrossing requires no special license, but the extreme left and right turns do require considerable skill to master. But the challenge is part of the fun. Entry fees are low, and even if you pop for a set of sticky race compound tires, they will last you many events. Autocrossing provides a fun, exciting, and challenging element of the sport for low cost and little time commitment.

World Challenge GT Class Nissan 2010. *Toyo Tire USA/SCCA Pro Racing*

Autocross requires an aggressive setup that puts heat in the tires quickly. An aggressive driving style helps, too. Here, Ken Motonishi is in his Mazda MX-5 S in San Diego. *Toyo Tire USA/Bryan Heitkotter*

Drag racing is great fun, but don't let the simplicity of the event fool you. Setup and tuning are just as important as in any other form of racing. *Toyo Tire USA*

## TIME TRIALS/TRACK DAY/TIME ATTACK

What may offer the most bang for the buck is the time trial. A time trial is an event on a road course with no wheel-to-wheel competition. While you are on the track with other cars, passing is allowed only on designated long straights. You must keep minimum distances between cars and car-to-car contact is strictly disallowed. You can easily reach racing speeds, but the damage and crash risk is greatly reduced compared to road racing. Events range from one to two days and typical track time is over one hour each day. Many groups around the country run time trials, so finding an event is easy. Track groups are run based on experience and car performance, so your daily driver sedan will not be on the track with a race-prepped super car. Many clubs have organized classes and lap times are taken with the fast time in class winning a trophy. And nearly every club or time trial group offers instruction

from experienced racers. These instructors often work for racing schools and they usually know their stuff, so the opportunity to learn is very high. Any kind of car is allowed, and modifications are no problem. Cars are teched prior to events and a helmet is required, along with a functional driver restraint. And some groups allow passengers, which adds an interesting element to the fun. Entry costs are low for the track time, tire wear is fairly high, and you can expect to accelerate the wear and tear on your machine, especially brakes, but it is hard to find a more fun way to play.

Time attacks are a little more intense, and can be very expensive. Drivers need experience to extract maximum performance from a car for a single lap, so many of the competitors are professionals. And the level of preparation is very high, since many companies use time attacks as a promotion for their products.

Bracket racing is the easiest form of drag racing from a setup point of view, but consistency is critical to successful elapsed times. *Hotchkis Sport Suspension*

**TRACK DRIVING OVERVIEW**

135

Keeping weight on the front end as long as possible during acceleration helps propel a front driver off a turn faster, as shown here by Tim Smith in a Honda. *Toyo Tire USA*

Muscle cars have never been known for handling, but Hotchkis has created suspension kits that turn these old behemoths into slot cars. They have used shock tuning to get weight onto the rear tires as fast as possible when accelerating off a turn, something that helps make these front-heavy tanks quick even on a tight autocross course. *Hotchkis Sport Suspension*

Muscle cars with handling packages come alive on faster tracks. This Hotchkis-equipped Camaro makes a great track car. *Hotchkis Sport Suspension*

The greatest element of a track day event is that lap times are not the point. Having fun is the priority, so you can spend a lot less time and money trying to chop that last second or two off of your lap time. And you can drive to and from the track with your track car. *Hotchkis Sport Suspension*

Time attack events have become immensely popular. JC Meynet's Subaru WRX set the track record at Las Vegas, but as you can see, these cars are very expensive. *Toyo Tire USA/JC Meynet*

Tire companies are very involved in time attack as a way to showcase their tires' performance. Toyo has been very successful with its Proxes R888. *Toyo Tire USA*

## RALLYING

Rallying comes in several flavors, ranging from a Friday or Saturday night skill/gimmick rally or navigation rally, to full-blown PRO Rallies with fully prepared rally cars and stiff competition. Skill/gimmick rallies are fun, challenging and easy. Usually run by local car clubs, these events require skill, but no special driving skills or car setup techniques are needed. Speed is not a factor as they are run on public roads with normal traffic and all traffic laws must be obeyed. This type of rally focuses on the driver and navigators' ability to read and follow often misleading route instructions.

Navigation rallies, which are also called time-speed-distance rallies, require a very precise ability; the driver and navigator must cover a specific section of the route in an exact time. Penalty points are given for every second of variation from the specified time. Covering a 35-minute segment of public roads and hitting the checkpoint at the exact second is a huge challenge. When you leave a checkpoint, your start time is recorded, and the same occurs when you reach the next checkpoint. In between, you follow a series of instructions (not a road map) to get from one checkpoint to the next. Not so easy. In a single evening event with five stages, the overall winner is often within 10 seconds of the minimum time. That is precision driving and navigating. Any kind of car will work and minimal equipment is needed for this type of event.

PRO Rally is an SCCA class based on top level rallying throughout the world. While this type of rally is also a time-speed-distance event, here many of the stages are on closed highways and forest roads and the allotted time for stages requires flat-out driving. In the United States, SCCA PRO rallies are run mostly on dirt forest roads and fully prepared cars are needed. This level of rallying is tremendous fun but also costly and time-consuming.

## RALLYCROSS

Rallycross is somewhat rare in the United States. A rallycross is simply an autocross on dirt. A tight, pylon course laid out on dirt requires good car control and some chassis setup, but otherwise nothing special equipment-wise.

## RALLYSPRINT

A rallysprint is also on dirt, or a combined dirt/asphalt course, but is a wheel-to-wheel event like road racing. These events are even more rare in the United States, but are held in some regions. Like road racing, rallysprint is more costly and time-consuming than rallycross.

## ROAD RACING

As Chef Emeril Lagasse would say, "It's time to kick it up a notch." If you like intensity, adrenaline, and a major test of skill, road racing is the way to fly. Nothing compares to the challenge presented by competing against a group of equally intense racers on a twisting, high-speed road circuit. It just doesn't get any better.

To go road racing requires a license, a car with required safety equipment, and a budget ranging from a few hundred dollars a race to several million if racing in the IndyCar Series is your cup of tea. At the club level, road racing, while not cheap, is affordable and not as difficult as many think. Getting involved is relatively easy. On a national level, the SCCA has regions throughout the country and classes for most cars. Other clubs conduct races on a regional level, like the National Auto Sport Association, which is expanding into several areas of the country, and the Race Car Club of America in the east.

The most challenging form of motorsports from a tuning standpoint is rallying. Cars must be set up for a wide variety of conditions, ranging from snow to sand to asphalt. Finding the optimum compromise is a real art form. *Eibach Springs*

Racing costs involve entry fees ranging from $200–$300 for a weekend, as well as maintenance and tires. For the stock type classes, a set of tires cost between $300 and $500 and a set will last for 3 to 7 weekends of racing. At the entry level, our GTi Cup VW Rabbit project car cost from $4,000 to $6,000 fully prepared. Without full safety equipment, your daily driver would not pass tech inspection for road racing like it would for a time trial. Not counting travel, you can race for as little as $400–$500 per weekend. While crashes occur, they are rare in club racing, and injuries are even more unusual. Considering the action, excitement, fun and challenge, the cost of road racing is relatively small.

## RACING SCHOOLS

The best way to get your feet wet in motorsports is by attending a racing school. They usually provide everything you need, including the car. In addition to the instruction provided, you will have the chance to find out how much you enjoy the activity before you invest in any equipment. And the school itself is fun and very cost-effective. When selecting a school, find out about the track time, damage liability, and prices before you register or make travel plans. Some comparison shopping can save you a lot of money and aggravation.

| | Import Drag Racing | Autocross/ Solo II | Rallying | Time Trials | Road Racing | Racing Schools |
|---|---|---|---|---|---|---|
| Ease of Participation | Easy | More Difficult | More Difficult | More Difficult | Difficult | Easy |
| Safety | Very Safe | Very Safe | Somewhat Dangerous (Public Roads) | Safe | Somewhat Dangerous (Wheel-To-Wheel Racing) | Safe |
| Vehicle Wear & Tear | Moderate | Moderate | Moderate | Moderately High | High | None |
| Cost to Participate | Low | Low | Low | Moderate | Moderate to High | Moderate to High |
| Track Time | Seconds/Day | Minutes /Day | Hours/Event | 1+ Hours/Day | 1+ Hours/Day | 1 to 3 Hours/Day |
| Maintenance Cost | Moderate | Moderate | Moderate to High | Moderate to High | Moderate to High | None |
| Maintenance Time | Moderate | Moderate | Moderate to High | Moderate to High | Moderate to High | None |
| Fun for Investment | Moderate | Moderate | Moderate to High | High | High | Moderate To High |
| Accessibility | Good | Excellent | Weak | Good | Good | Good |
| Potential Car Damage | Low | Very Low | High | Moderate | High | None |
| Car Preperation Cost | Zero to Very High | Low | Zero to Low | Moderate | High | None |

This chart provides a comparison of various forms of motorsports.

Club racing with SCCA and NASA is great fun. The wide variety of classes and spec racing opportunities can make the cost manageable. The setup challenges for road racing are very different than a time trial, autocross, or time attack, where one lap is all that matters. In road racing, finding a car setup and driving style that allows maximum tire traction for the duration of the event is much more difficult than a setup for a single fast lap. *Toyo Tire USA*

# Index

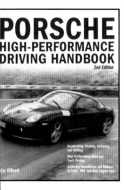
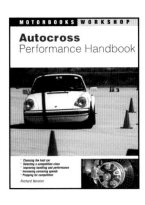
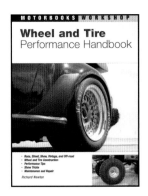
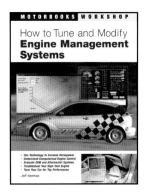
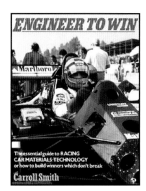